Fun "In Store" For Students

A Step-By-Step Curriculum Integrated Resource And Activity Book For Developing, Operating, And Integrating A School Store Or A School Based Business Into An Elementary Or Junior High School. Also Included In This Book Are Assembly Plans To Build The Biggest, Most Durable, Self Locking, Continuous Fundraising, Mobile School Store And A Hands-On "Real-Life" Financial Literacy Section.

Endorsements

"The students had so much fun developing and operating their own store. We used a mobile school store like the one in this book. We sold things in different locations and made a lot of money to buy needed supplies and equipment for our school"—Barb Born . . . . Family and Consumer Education Teacher

"There were so many reproducible pages that I could immediately use when starting the school store and then in the classroom. The hands-on activities, resources, and the consumer math section opened my student's eyes to how school work relates to career work and the math associated with real-life living. Also, my students learned a lot of employability skills. The worker maturity self-evaluations, worker maturity teacher evaluations, and tests advanced their worker maturity skills early in life"—Carrie King, M.S. . . . . Occupational Teacher

"I like the way the book was presented and organized. I could easily navigate through the appendices to find what I was looking for. The lesson plans and curriculum integration ideas gave me more tools and resources to help us achieve our goals and objectives"—Cassandra Chaney, M.S . . . . Resource Coordinator

Fun
“In Store”
For Students

Fun "In Store" For Students

BY

Chad B. Klapper, M.S.

---

iUniverse, Inc.
Bloomington

Fun "In Store" For Students

iUniverse books may be ordered through booksellers or by contacting:

iUniverse
1663 Liberty Drive
Bloomington, IN 47403
www.iuniverse.com
1-800-Authors (1-800-288-4677)

ISBN: 978-1-4620-4308-8 (sc)
ISBN: 978-1-4620-4309-5 (ebk)

Library of Congress Control Number: 2011913703

Printed in the United States of America

iUniverse rev. date: 01/17/2012

To My Daughter . . .

There's no telling what you can do when you get inspired by goals.
There's no telling what you can do when you believe in goals.
There's no telling what will happen when you act upon goals.
Ninety percent of education is encouragement.

There are many reasons why you or your school may want to develop and operate a school store or a school-based business. These reasons may include providing your school with a continuous fundraiser, meeting academic standards, developing employability skills, providing students with interesting and exciting work experiences, maximizing academic success by connecting school-to-work, integrating school and work-based learning, or increasing awareness of careers in business including entrepreneurship. Whatever the reasons, a school store or school-based business has many features and benefits.

This resource and activity book is centered on a school store but this book can also be used for other school based businesses. I believe a school store, which requires the practical application of general employment and academic skills to real life work situations, provides an excellent opportunity for elementary and junior high/middle school students to begin developing the skills needed to succeed in the world of work.

As an added bonus, students who have worked at the school store have reported it to be a "fun experience." In other words, students can begin developing skills, and have fun doing it.

Further, I believe that the students who work at these school-based businesses become more responsible and gain numerous "work-based learning experiences" they otherwise might wait years to obtain. These work-based experiences are reproducible and can be integrated into a supervised program by having students work at a school store, or other entrepreneurial ventures.

These young entrepreneurs also improve their communication skills and benefit by learning about the value of customer service. The students develop an appreciation for the value of work. Understanding the value of work and its rewards helps the students understand the concept of goals.

This is why I developed and operated school stores in the school districts where I taught. When I experienced the benefits from a school based business, from hand-on activities, and from hands-on processes, I began to share them with other school districts. The feedback I received from the other school districts encouraged me to create this book and share it with as many schools, educators, facilitators, and students as I can.

I would like to thank my fellow teachers, students, advisors, coordinators, parents, PTA's, community businesses, and friends for their inspiration and words of encouragement.

Every effort has been made to ascertain proper ownership of copyrighted materials and to cite references and/or obtain permission for their use. Any omission is unintentional.

TABLE OF CONTENTS

INTRODUCTION

Fun "In Store" For Students is a resource and activity book to help teachers and/or facilitators develop, operate, and/or justify a school store. There are many activities, resources, lessons, assessments, evaluations, and reproducible pages. This book is centered on a school store but it can be used for other school-based businesses.

Section 1 is a suggested sequence for developing and operating a school store. This section, like other sections, has you turning to different appendices located in the back of the book. These appendices are used as resources, activities, supplemental material, and informational purposes during the 'developing and operating' process. During the 'developing and operating' process, ideas and examples are given to integrate some of the activities and processes into your classroom.

Section 2 lists the Wisconsin academic performance and content standards that can be achieved by operating a school store, depending on your scope and goals. These examples may be used as a template for meeting standards in your state. Each state has its own unique standards and competencies. These unique standards and competencies may be used to both "develop and justify" a school store or other school based business ventures.

Section 3 has you start thinking about forming business and education partnerships. A school store or school based business is an excellent opportunity for you, your students, or the school to form partnerships with local or regional businesses. With a little networking and communication, the business and education partnerships are endless. Partnerships promote better education, develop a better-trained work force, and strengthen the learning process by improving communication and understanding between schools and communities.

Section 4 is the financial literacy section. This section is a useful tool because it opens student's eyes to additional authentic hands-on learning that connects school work with career work/awareness, and the math associated with real-life living. This section, "turns on the light bulb," to the real-world process of establishing a monthly budget and being a consumer. Students experience actual things they are going to encounter soon in their lives. Consumer math is an excellent spiral for integrating employment (like at the school store), with authentic living.

Section 5 contains the appendices where you find most of your resources, supplemental materials, lesson plans, activities, assessments, evaluations, and reproducible pages to be used by the students and facilitators of the school store.

Section 6 contains assembly plans for the biggest, most durable, self-locking, continuous fundraising mobile school store. There are many reasons why a school may want to develop and operate a school store, or better, a mobile school store. Maybe your school wants a continuous fundraiser with access to a variety of locations and customers, and easy self-locking storage. Maybe your school is interested in providing students with interesting and exciting work experiences that promote lifelong learning, and maximizing academic success by connecting school to work. Whatever the reasons, a mobile school store has many features and benefits.

Section 7 contains additional resources to investigate. Vendors with school supplies, resource sites for teachers, and entrepreneurial addresses are a few of the wonderful resources in this section. These sites also have other links that may be useful to you.

The developmental and operational processes for your school store may vary from school to school depending on your school's size, your goals, and your objectives for running a store. Some sample goals or objectives include:

- Meeting academic standards
- Having a continuous fundraiser
- Developing employability skills
- Developing job-seeking skills
- Developing financial literacy skills
- Integrating school and work-based learning
- Expanding awareness of careers in business, including entrepreneurship
- Developing partnerships involving school/business/community members

SECTION 1

DEVELOPING AND OPERATING A SCHOOL STORE

INTRODUCTION

There are two different avenues you and/or your school can travel when developing and operating a school store.

The first avenue is using your school store strictly as a fundraiser. For example, maybe your goal is to use the mobile school store from section six as a continuous fundraiser to sell snacks in the cafeteria, in the hallway, at sporting events in the gym, or during outside events and activities. If that is your goal, then the procedure for developing and operating that store is going to be different than if your goal is to integrate the store's development and operations into parts of your curriculum. If your goal is strictly fundraising, your developmental and operational process is relatively easy. All you need to do for this avenue is to get administrative approval, buy the supplies to build the school store, build the store, stock the store with snacks and/or merchandise, price the stocked items, and then determine your locations and times to sell your items. Some schools may not need a mobile store because they already have the ability to sell merchandise by using a table, a room, or other means. If that is the case, developing and operating a school store becomes easier yet. Whatever the scenario, the individuals involved in the development and operating process of a school store, for fundraising purposes only, may only include a few faculty members or a few students to help sell the snacks and merchandise at various locations and times. You may not have to do a bunch of hiring, orientating, developing a business plan, or thinking about other things. However, it is still suggested that you at least read all the topics in this section, along with appendix A, "School Store Business Plans," to get a more holistic perspective of ideas and examples. Further, the depth and scope of each topic in Section 1 and in Appendix A will also be determined by your goals and objectives for developing and operating a school store.

The second avenue is integrating the school store's development, operations, activities, and concepts into the classrooms and parts of your curriculum as you begin to develop and operate the store. The following pages are a suggested sequence for achieving the goals of integrating the school store's development, operations, concepts, and activities into the classrooms and parts of your curriculum, as well as being a continuous fundraiser. The first three steps to this process are administrative approval, faculty involvement, and hiring. After administrative approval and faculty involvement, hiring is next so that the students become involved right away in the developmental process of starting a school store. The student's early involvement will maximize the benefits a school store has to offer them.

ADMINISTRATIVE APPROVAL

Coordinators of the school store may want to contact administration. By communicating with the administration right away, you may avoid conflicts. Talk to your administration or supervisor about the features, the benefits, and the goals of the school store. Also, you may want to mention setting up an optional school store committee that administration or your supervisor can be a member of. The amount of administrative involvement will vary from school to school, depending on your scope and goals.

FACULTY INVOLVEMENT (optional school store committee)

A school store committee of a few people may or may not be needed. However, some of the responsibility, work, and communication that are involved with coordinating the store might be more evenly distributed. The committee's members could include students, teachers, parents, PTO's, administrators, and businesses. Some or all of the committee decisions may need to go through administrative approval. With teachers on the committee, important issues that teachers may be concerned about can be discussed and potential conflicts can be avoided. These potential conflicts include where and when the store should be open, items not allowed in the classrooms, items to sell, fundraising conflicts, funds needed to start a school store, and/or other entrepreneurial ideas. It is a good idea to network and communicate as much as possible. For example, suppose a fellow staff member is trying to do some fundraising for needed equipment by selling candy bars during the month of December. If the school store sells candy bars in December, the store would be in direct competition with the other staff member. That situation may cause a potential conflict. The amount of faculty involvement will vary from school to school, depending on your scope and goals.

Once these initial steps and/or concerns are relatively addressed, then let the fun "in store" for students begin by doing some hiring of employees. The hiring process for the school store is flexible.

HIRING

Hiring can be a relatively simple process, or hiring can be a more holistic process. The depth and scope of the hiring process will vary from school to school, depending on your needs and goals. If a relatively simple hiring process meets your goals and needs, then you can determine whatever process works best for you. There are many hiring processes.

If a more holistic process meets your needs when determining your goals, objectives, employability skills, and/or academic standards that you would like to incorporate; you may want to include activities that pertain to ads, job applications, and interviewing. That is usually the way the "finding employment" process works in the "real world." You read or hear about an ad that some company or business is hiring. You go pick up a job application, complete the application, and return the application. Then, you wait to get contacted to see if you have an interview or to see if you have been denied the job.

Ads

Figure 1-1

There are many ways to advertise that the school store is "now hiring." For example, you could make announcements over the P.A. and inform students of where they can pick up job applications and where and when they need to be returned. Another way to let students become aware of school store employment opportunities is to post flyers on bulletin boards or on walls around the school. Further, you could put a flyer in each teacher's mailbox or send an email to the teachers to have all the teachers "mention" or talk about school store employment opportunities in homeroom or in one of their classes. You may want a place where job applications can always be found for job openings at the store or other in-school businesses. There are many ways to distribute your desired information. Figure 1-1 is an example of a local advertisement for a cashier.

Job Applications

Figure 1-2

APPLICATION FOR EMPLOYMENT

DATE ______

WE CONSIDER APPLICANTS FOR ALL POSITIONS WITHOUT REGARD TO RACE, COLOR, RELIGION, SEX, NATIONAL ORIGIN, AGE, MARITAL OR VETERAN STATUS, THE PRESENCE OF NON-JOB RELATED MEDICAL CONDITION OR DISABILITY, OR ANY OTHER LEGALLY PROTECTED STATUS.

PERSONAL

NAME First Middle Last

ADDRESS: Street City State Zip Area Code Telephone

POSITION APPLIED FOR | SALARY DESIRED | DATE AVAILABLE | DO YOU PREFER ☐ FULL TIME ☐ PART TIME | ANY LIMITATION ON HOURS OR DAYS ☐ YES ☐ NO

Have you ever worked for this company before? ☐ YES ☐ No, If so, where

Do you presently have relatives working for us? ☐ YES ☐ No, If yes, give ______ Name ______ Relation ______ Location

Are you 18 years of age or older? ☐ YES ☐ No, If not, your birthdate: __/__/__

Have you ever been discharged from any position? ☐ YES ☐ No, If yes, give reason

Have you ever been convicted of a crime other than a minor traffic violation? (Having been convicted will not necessarily prevent a person from employment) ☐ YES ☐ No, If yes, give reason

Are you currently employed? ☐ YES ☐ No

Are you prevented from lawfully becoming employed in this country because of Visa or Immigration status? ☐ YES ☐ No (Proof of citizenship or immigration status will be required upon employment.)

HOW DID YOU LEARN ABOUT US?

☐ ADVERTISEMENT ☐ FRIEND ☐ WALK-IN
☐ EMPLOYMENT AGENCY ☐ RELATIVE ☐ OTHER ______

EDUCATION

SCHOOL	NAME	LOCATION	COMPLETED	GRADUATED	COURSE OR MAJOR
Elementary			Circle 5 6 7 8	☐ YES ☐ NO	
High School			1 2 3 4	☐ YES ☐ NO	
College			1 2 3 4	☐ YES ☐ NO	
Other (Specify)				☐ YES ☐ NO	

HOURS AVAILABLE

	SUNDAY	MONDAY	TUESDAY	WEDNESDAY	THURSDAY	FRIDAY	SATURDAY
FROM:							
TO:							

MILITARY

BRANCH	DATE ENTERED	DATE SEPARATED	PRESENT OR LAST RANK

SPECIAL SKILLS OR TRAINING

Revised 10/96

WE ARE AN EQUAL OPPORTUNITY EMPLOYER

The job applications, along with other materials and resources, are located in Appendix B. There are two applications. One is designed more for an elementary level student and one is designed for junior high students. The applications can be modified to meet your needs. The concept of filling out an application is more important than which application you use or how you may modify the applications. Figure 1-2 is an example of a local grocery store's application for employment.

When the students are completing the job applications, they may worry about "past work experiences and/or references." You can tell them that all experience is valuable, even babysitting and helping mom and dad with household chores. In many cases, these are the only work experiences that students will have. These experiences say something about the student's ability to handle responsibility and follow directions.

There are additional materials and resources in appendix B and appendix F that you may want to consider addressing with your students/workers. The additional materials and resources in appendix B include an Application Checklist, an Interview Checklist, and an Interview Test. The additional resources in appendix F include Worker Maturity Employee Performance Evaluations (the student's self evaluation and a teacher evaluation of the student/worker) for elementary and junior high students, a Worker Maturity Test, and an Understanding Labor Market Information Test. Appendix F centers on evaluations and tests of worker maturity skills **after** being employed, but you may want the students to know these skills in advance.

Depending on your time, scope, and goals, the additional resources and materials do not have to be distributed and/or discussed right away. There are many options available. For example, you can orally discuss the related materials or you can hand them out separately. Further, the additional resources and materials could be attached (stapled) to the application to help students prepare for school store interviews, they could be distributed at another time, or they don't have to be distributed/discussed at all. The additional resources and materials are supplemental materials included to help students realize some of the real-life expectations and interview processes that they may encounter in the future.

After receiving the returned applications, and before you interview, it is time to decide which student workers most fulfill your needs, depending on your scope and goals. The workers do not have to be limited to the highest achieving students. The school store staff could include special needs students as well. Not all positions require strong academic abilities. Some positions focus on advertising, setting up merchandise, taking inventories, making purchasing decisions, and more. These are tasks that allow students with a wide range of abilities to become involved. In addition to these student populations, the store could involve reluctant learners, underachievers, and others who are at risk of failing. Another example is the school store could be, for example, a fourth grade project. All fourth graders would then apply and interview for a position at the store. All the fourth graders may not be hired, or even needed, but at least they would have been exposed to the hiring process early in their lives.

Interviews
Next, you may want to schedule interviews and inform students when and where they will be interviewed. Choose appropriate questions at the student's level of comprehension. You may want to use open-ended questions and encourage students to "sell themselves."

Following the interviewing process, select those students who most appropriately fulfill your needs. You may want to mention or include a probation period, like most jobs have in the "real-world."

These activities and processes can be modified to meet your needs. Whatever hiring process you choose will be extremely informative and beneficial to students this early in their developmental stages.

ORIENTATION

Once you have selected some or all of the employees, meet with them to discuss and answer questions they may have. If there is not a lot of orientation time available, some topics can be mentioned and then handouts can be distributed. The importance, number of topics discussed, and time in orientation will vary from school to school depending on your scope and goals. If you are given the time you need to meet with your new employees before opening the business, it would be ideal to discuss general guidelines, employability skills and attitudes, job descriptions, and do a business plan.

General Guidelines—General guidelines might cover cash box operation, work schedules, employee conduct, dress code, professionalism, responsibility, dependability, teamwork, discount policy, and many other topics. These guidelines will vary from store to store depending on your scope and goals. A starting point for developing your own policies and/or guidelines is found in appendix C. You may want to include the store employees, committee members, or other students when developing general guidelines.

Employability Skills and Attitudes—These are skills and attitudes needed to obtain and retain general employment. Appendix D begins by describing the components of employability skills and attitudes, which were excerpted from Education for Employment. Appendix D also has two references. School store facilitators may want to read and/or discuss the two references in appendix D.

Reference 1 is data and quotes from surveyed Wisconsin employers and states reasons why students were not initially hired. The survey, data, and quotes from Wisconsin employers are dated. However, I believe the reasons mentioned can still be applied and characterized in today's workplace. Also, even though the data came from Wisconsin employers, I believe this data is applicable to many states and students, and not just Wisconsin. Further, I like the way this data was organized and presented. It included specific quotes, ideas, concepts, and categories that can be interpreted and understood easier by students and facilitators of a school store.

Reference 2 was excerpted from the internet. This article was part of "Preparing Youth for Employable Futures," by E.C. Needleman. This research is more recent. The goals and concepts parallel that of Education for Employment. You can discuss one article, both articles, or parts of each article, depending on your scope and goals.

Job Descriptions—The job descriptions may vary based on the needs of your store and age of your students. Appendix E lists some job descriptions for a school store. Keep in mind that students may need time to grow into these positions. Also, several students may be needed for any one position. School store advisors can assist by training students and by performing those tasks that may be, at first, too difficult for students to perform. Situations and scheduling may arise where it is not possible to have specific job titles. If that happens, employees can work as a team. The job titles may be modified to meet the goals of your store.

DEVELOPING A BUSINESS PLAN AND OPENING YOUR STORE

The next thing you may want to do with your students and/or the school store committee is create some sort of business plan. A business plan is an overview of the business. The depth and scope of the business plan will vary from school to school, depending on your scope and goals.

Components of a Business Plan

- Market analysis
- Potential customers
- Business name and type of business (manufacturer, retailer, service provider)
- Bookkeeping (business records)
- Staffing
- Location
- Equipment, supplies needed, and suppliers
- Competition
- Pricing
- Advertising
- Funds needed to open for business

The Reasons and Functions for Writing a Business Plan

- Provides entrepreneurs (students) with a road map that they need in order to run their business
- Assists in financing decisions
- Helps entrepreneurs clearly think through what type of business they are starting and allows them to consider every aspect of the business process
- Raises the questions that need to be answered in order to succeed in business
- Establishes a system of checks and balances
- Sets benchmarks to keep the business in control
- Helps to develop a competitive spirit
- It gives the entrepreneurs a "go" or "no go" answer about starting the business
- Serves as a management tool by which a company's (school store) progress can be measured and monitored

The complexity and detail of your business plan will depend on if your store is going to be used as a continuous fundraiser only, or if your store's development and operations are going to be integrated into parts of the curriculum, along with being used as a continuous fundraiser.
Further, you may not even address some of the components of a business plan because they have already been addressed or are not needed because of your scope and goals.

There are three different examples of business plans in appendix A. The first business plan is called "Simple Business Plan (Elementary)." You may want to use this business plan if you are incorporating younger students into the development of your store or if you are just using the store as a continuous fundraiser.

The second business plan is called "Simple Business Plan (Junior High). You may want to use this business plan if you are incorporating junior high aged students into the development of your store, or if you are just using the store as a continuous fundraiser.

The third business plan is called "Detailed Business Plan for a School Store." The detailed business plan has specific examples and ideas for operating a school store and is centered on integrating the store's development and operations into parts of your curriculum. The detailed business plan process can be used at any grade level. However, depending on the age of your students, some portions of the process may have to be modified. The ideas and examples in each component of the detailed business plan come from feedback from other schools, school store coordinators, and me.

Whatever business plan you choose, you may want to complete, or at least consider, every question/component of that business plan to give you a more holistic view of your direction, procedure, and goals. If you decide to use one of the "Simple Business Plans" you may want to take a look at the "Detailed Business Plan for a School Store" to acquire other possible ideas that the "Simple Business Plans" may not describe in detail.

Further, if your goal is to integrate the store's development and operations into parts of the curriculum, then ideally it would be great to have as many students as possible develop a business plan to expand their awareness in starting a business. However, availability 'at one time' with all the students that are involved with the school store may not be as feasible as you would like. If time and availability are factors, there are other options. For example, the students could be given business plan handouts to brainstorm and hand in at a later time. Or, business plan handouts can be given to students to brainstorm and then have one meeting, with as many students as possible, to network and develop the foundation of the business plan.

Depending on your scope and goals, the business plans could be integrated into social studies classes, language arts classes, math classes, business classes, marketing classes, and other areas. Advisors may want to modify or create their own business plan questions depending on your business, your time, the age of your students, and your goals.

Once you and/or the store committee decide on which avenue your school store is going to take, then develop your business plan, open your store, and start making money.

MONITORING THE SCHOOL STORE

Now that your business has been operating and developing, it is time to troubleshoot any situations. By now you probably have felt some of the "bumps" that have presented themselves. The manager, employees, you, and/or the committee can brainstorm and take action to alleviate any concerns the school, administration, teachers, employees, or customers are having. Work as a team. Remember, "light is the task when many share the toil." In other words, many hands make light work.

As you monitor the store, you may want/need to adjust/alter some of your goals and/or objectives. Whatever the situation, the school store's development and operations are very flexible. The depth and scope of monitoring the store will vary from school to school, depending on your goals.

ASSESSMENT AND EVALUATION OF YOUR WORKERS

Advisors may complete periodic worker maturity performance evaluations for each student employed at the school store so students will have an opportunity to improve their work performance. It may be a good procedure to ask students to first evaluate themselves. Positive feedback and strategies for improving are an important part of the evaluation. The worker maturity performance evaluations, worker maturity tests, and understanding the labor market information test in appendix F, can be used as they are or changed to reflect the workplace competencies, goals, and skills that have been chosen for your students. The evaluations and tests that have been included in this book are for student self-evaluation, teacher evaluation, and informational purposes. These evaluations and tests are real-life examples of the situations and thinking processes the students may encounter in the "world of work." The depth and scope of assessment and evaluation will vary from school to school, depending on your goals.

FUTURE OF THE SCHOOL STORE OR OTHER ENTREPRENEURIAL VENTURES

Teachers and facilitators in elementary or junior high schools can help students understand the opportunities of our entrepreneurial economy by infusing entrepreneurship related activities into the school, such as a school store or other school based businesses. The activities can encourage students to think creatively and not just determine how businesses operate now. Help them ask questions about how businesses might be created in new and better ways, using new and different processes. Open their eyes to the entrepreneurial opportunities that are around us. Help them ask questions about expanding the current business by having new/different products and/or services. Talk about applying strategies for creating assets, defining and creating a savings, and defining and creating some investments. Activities will enable students to complete some or all of the components of entrepreneurship education.

Components of Entrepreneurship Education

- Define entrepreneur and entrepreneurship
- Describe the three types of businesses
- Establish goals for a classroom business
- List the components of a business plan
- Develop a business plan for a class business
- Develop and operate a classroom business

Entrepreneur

An entrepreneur is an individual who takes risks, organizes, and manages a business or industrial enterprise, with the hope of making a profit. Regardless of what they sell and how much money they earn, many entrepreneurs share characteristics such as confidence, perseverance, vision, drive, adaptability, competitiveness, honesty, creativity, and the willingness to take risks.

Entrepreneurship

Entrepreneurship is the process of planning and organizing a business or enterprise.

Ideas for Entrepreneurship with the Three Types of Businesses

Figure 1-3

- *Manufacturers*—These businesses manufacture products that they sell to retailers or directly to their customers. Examples of products that students could manufacture are greeting cards, Christmas/holiday ornaments, coloring books, gift boxes, hand crafted items, buttons, silk-screened tee shirts and hats, food products, plants, and many more.
- *Retailers*—These businesses usually do not manufacture goods. They buy their products and resell them to consumers at a profit. Examples of products that students could buy and then sell for a profit are school supplies, food products, tee shirts, caps, buttons, handmade crafts, and many more.
- *Services*—These businesses provide services to their customers rather than products. Examples of services that students could provide are tutoring (computer skills, foreign language, sports skills, musical instruments, etc.), gift wrapping, baby sitting, letter writing and mailing service, in-school deliveries, printing service (customized stationary, greeting cards, announcements, and other printing services), entertainment (magic show, music, and clowns), car cleaning service, party service, organize garage sales, and many more. Figure 1-3 is an example of a local schools yearly car washing fundraiser.

Sample Goals for a Classroom Business

- Acquaint students with the skills and personal qualities small business owners need to succeed
- Provide an ongoing extra curricular enrichment program during school hours
- Provide educational enrichment that is self-funded
- Foster a work ethic in the school community
- Foster partnerships between parents, teachers, and the community
- Create an opportunity for a school based work program

Small Businesses Are a Big Factor

Small businesses in the United States provide nearly half of the private sector payroll and half of the private sector jobs. In the fourth quarter of 2009, small business national Gross Domestic Product grew by 5.7 percent. That is why small businesses are considered a cornerstone to a healthy economy. Wisconsin, for example, mirrors the nation with nearly 500,000 small businesses that employ more than half of all workers in the state.

Expanding Awareness of Careers in Business, Including Entrepreneurship

Classroom Enterprises (Entrepreneurship)
"Tomorrow's Entrepreneur's Are In Our Classrooms Today"

For today's school students, there are many new and exciting programs in the transition from school to work. This involves the integration of academic and vocational education programs that are the talk of vocational education leadership today. Preparing all segments of the population to make the United States more competitive in the world economy means better preparation to get a job and move up the career ladder in a technologically advanced society.

Preparation for a job, to be a better worker, and to please the employer is our entire focus. But, who is preparing the employer? And who decides if you are going to get a job or start a business? The opportunity to create your own job is sadly missing in most of the plans for these transition and apprenticeship messages published today. Yet, it applies to every conceivable technology being addressed in our school system.

Research shows that a majority of the small business owners in the U.S. have little or no advanced education, but they are an important part of today's employers and will continue to be the entrepreneurs creating the jobs of the future. Ask them if entrepreneurship should be a critical part of today's educational system, a part of every technical preparation and work experience program. Our country is not, nor ever was, completely made up of large corporations like Ford, IBM, and Proctor & Gamble, and we cannot focus our education only on providing workers for jobs in mammoth companies, particularly now that they are scaling down to be able to compete in global markets. To be competitive, we must value the small and flexible business and teach our students to be part of that world, too.

Entrepreneurship concepts and courses should be valued as part of every transition from school to work programs for the following reasons.

- Job opportunities in small business require a much broader knowledge of the operations of a business, not just a technical skill
- We owe all Americans an exposure to the opportunity to start a business, especially when they may find that jobs are scarce
- Entrepreneurship education suggests a career option that can empower our disadvantaged and under-motivated youth and adults in a world where jobs seem to be shrinking
- Entrepreneurship is active learning that develops thinking skills of all kinds in relation to real business issues
- Entrepreneurship is a support course for all technologies
- The entrepreneurial spirit is an orientation to change and innovation that serves all types of businesses well in a competitive economy
- Many Americans use their technical skills to create a business and sometimes fail because they never learned how to run a business.

Reprinted/excerpted from EntrepreNews & Views: A New Venture in Vocational Education. Winter 1994. Vol. 4, No. 1. International Consortium for Entrepreneurship Education. *Center on Education and Training for Employment, The Ohio State University, 1900 Kenny Road, Columbus, Ohio 43210-1090*

SECTION 2

ACHIEVING ACADEMIC STANDARDS WITH THE INTEGRATION OF A SCHOOL STORE

INTRODUCTION

Teachers and/or facilitators are great resources for ideas for learning activities and sometimes, they don't even know it. There are many classroom activities, standards, and concepts that can be achieved with the integration of a school store. These activities, standards, and concepts can be spread across the curriculum with a team of teachers, or they can be achieved individually, depending on your scope and goals.

ACHIEVING ACADEMIC STANDARDS WITH THE INTEGRATION OF A SCHOOL STORE

Besides the national standards, each state has its own unique standards and competencies. These unique state standards and competencies may be used to both "develop and justify" a school store. There are many standards and competencies, in all states, that can be achieved by integrating a school store program. It all depends on your scope, goals, and which content areas you are comfortable integrating.

For example, one of California's mathematics standards for fourth grade statistics, data analysis, and probability is "Students organize, represent, and interpret numerical and categorical data and clearly communicate their findings: 1.1 Formulate survey questions; systematically collect and represent data on a number line; and coordinate graphs, tables, and charts. Another example is one of Maine's English Language Arts standards. The standard reads: "E. Processes of Writing and Speaking—Students will demonstrate the ability to use the skills and strategies of the writing process. *Effective communication can improve the work of writers and speakers. Students will use a wide range of strategies to address different audiences for a variety of purposes. Students will write or speak for reflective, creative, and informational purposes.*" A school store program can be used to help meet these two performance standard examples from California and Maine (see Appendix G).

Further, the state of Wisconsin no longer has restricted its academic standards to the four core areas of English/Language Arts, Mathematics, Science, and Social Studies. The other Wisconsin Model Academic Standards include seventeen additional areas. These education areas include agricultural, art and design, business, dance, environmental, family & consumer, foreign language, health, information & technology literacy, marketing, music, personal financial literacy, physical education, school counseling, technology, theatre, and world languages. Additionally, in Wisconsin, districts are aligning their curriculum and K-12 performance standards with state standards, which in turn, are aligned with the objectives on the WKCE (Wisconsin Knowledge and Concepts Exam). The WKCE is the state assessment that is administered in grades 3-8, and 10.

The following are two examples of content and performance standards from Wisconsin. These standards are centered on the school store used in this book. These examples may also be used as a possible template to develop, justify, facilitate, and/or achieve state performance and state content standards in your state.

The examples are how some of the performance standards for Business and Marketing may be achieved with the use of your school store. These two examples are used to help you get used to referencing Wisconsin state performance standards, cross referencing state performance standards, and symbolism.

The following performance standards may be achieved through the integration of a school store, through some of the activities in appendix G, and by using some of the ideas in this book when developing and operating a school store.

The information contained in the parentheses after each performance standard is a cross reference to a similar core performance standard. Please use the following when cross-referencing:

LA = Language Arts
M = Mathematics
SC = Science
SS = Social Studies

Example 1

Standards Booklet: Business
Content Standard: Students in Wisconsin will communicate in a clear, courteous, concise, and correct manner on personal and professional levels.
Performance Standard: A.4.5 Compose a standard business letter (see LA B.4.1, B.4.2)

In example one, performance standard A.4.5 in Business is cross-referenced to two core English Language Arts (LA) performance standards. The two core English Language Arts performance standards are:
LA B.4.1 Create or produce writing to communicate with different audiences for a variety of purposes
LA B.4.2 Plan, revise, edit, and publish clear and effective writing

Example 2

Standards Booklet: Marketing Education
Content Standard: Students in Wisconsin will assess the essential role of entrepreneurship ventures within the free enterprise system
Performance Standard: A.4.3 Participate in an entrepreneurial venture; e.g., school-based business (see SS D.4.1, D.4.2, D.4.4; LA E.4.3)

In example two, Marketing Education performance standard A.4.3 is cross-referenced to three Social Studies (SS) performance standards, and one English Language Arts (LA) performance standard. Those "core" performance standards are as follows:
SS D.4.1 Describe and explain the role of money, banking, and savings in everyday life.
SS D.4.2 Identify situations requiring an allocation of limited economic resources and appraise the opportunity cost (for example, spending one's allowance on a movie will mean less money saved for a new bike)
SS D.4.4 Give examples to explain how business and industry depend upon workers with specialized skills to make production more efficient
LA E.4.3 Create products appropriate to audience and purpose

- Write news articles appropriate for familiar media
- Create simple advertising messages and graphics appropriate to familiar media
- Prepare, perform, and tape simple radio and television scripts
- Prepare and perform school announcements and program scripts

POTENTIALLY ACHIEVED WISCONSIN STATE STANDARDS WITH INTEGRATION OF A SCHOOL STORE

Depending on the depth and scope of your school store integration, the following is where the school store's concepts and activities can integrate into many of the State of Wisconsin Department of Public Instruction (DPI) Standards. Cross-referencing is also included in parenthesis. These standards may parallel standards in other states.

Business

A. Communications

By the end of grade 4 students will:
Written Communications
A.4.1 Demonstrate correct spelling, grammar, word usage, and legible writing (see LA B.4.3)
A.4.2 Write, edit, and revise an original creative work incorporating correct spelling, grammar, and punctuation (see LA B.4.2)
A.4.3 Compose simple requests for information (see LA B.4.1)
A.4.4 Take simple notes (see LA F.4.1)
A.4.5 Compose a standard business letter (see LA B.4.1, B.4.2)

Oral Communications
A.4.6 Express wants, needs, and feelings (see LA C.4.3)
A.4.7 Demonstrate the difference between opinion and fact (see LA C.4.2)
A.4.8 Participate in group discussion and role-playing (see LA C.4.1)
A.4.9 Demonstrate telephone etiquette
A.4.10 Follow oral directions (see LA C.4.2)
A.4.11 Demonstrate the ability to listen for meaning (see LA C.4.2)
A.4.12 Record complete and accurate messages and notes (see LA B.4.1)

Workplace Communications
A.4.13 Give and follow simple instructions (see LA B.4.1, C.4.1, C.4.2)
A.4.14 Greet people appropriately in a variety of situations (see LA D.4.2)
A.4.15 Take turns communicating in a group situation (see LA C.4.1, C.4.3)
A.4.16 Deliver informal appreciation messages in a variety of situations (see LA D.4.2, B.4.1)
A.4.17 Make a written/oral request (see LA D.4.2)

By the end of grade 8 students will:
Written Communications
A.8.1 Write, edit, and revise business correspondence, outlines, summaries, and reports using correct grammar, mechanics, and word usage (see LA B.8.1, B.8.2)

A.8.5 Plan, draft, and revise a spontaneous piece that demonstrates effective language use, structure, style, and correctness (see B.8.2)

Oral Communications
A.8.6 Present brief impromptu remarks pertaining to topics of current or general interest (see LA C.8.1)
A.8.7 Research and present a speech relating to career choices (see LA C.8.1)
A.8.8 Ask appropriate questions when more information is needed (see LA C.8.3)
A.8.9 Demonstrate and interpret nonverbal cues (see LA C.8.3)
A.8.10 Demonstrate respect for differences in regional and multicultural communication (see LA C.8.1, D.8.2)

Workplace Communications
A.8.11 Identify and define the components of the communication process (see LA C.8.2)
A.8.12 Identify barriers to communication
A.8.13 Make introductions in a variety of situations
A.8.14 Describe the steps of problem-solving negotiation
A.8.15 Describe the characteristics of an effective team
A.8.16 Write a thank-you letter

B. Information Systems/Technology

Business students will:
B.BS.5 Use data to create information to solve business problems
B.BS.6 Use desktop publishing software to design, create, and produce a variety of publications (see LA E.8.3)
B.BS.8 Use multimedia software to design, create, and produce a variety of presentations (see LA E.8.3)

By the end of grade 8 students will:
B. 8.7 Use spreadsheet software to create, store, retrieve, update, and delete data

C. Financial Procedures

By the end of grade 4 students will:
C.4.1 Recognize different denominations of currency and coins (see M B.4.3)
C.4.2 Identify the value of each denomination (see M D.4.4)
C.4.3 Calculate mathematics problems requiring adding, subtracting, multiplying, and dividing different denominations (see M B.4.5)
C.4.3 Estimate mathematical calculations

By the end of grade 8 students will:
C.8.1 Calculate sales tax (see M B.8.5)
C.8.2 Make change in a sales transaction
C.8.3 Determine the amount of savings needed for a short-term goal
C.8.4 Verify the accuracy of financial calculations

D. Economics

By the end of grade 4 students will:
D.4.2 Define economic wants and explain how they are satisfied (see SS D.4.2)
D.4.3 Identify factors that can influence the prices of goods and services

By the end of grade 8 students will:
D.8.5 Apply economic concepts to consumer decision making, buying, saving, and investing (see SS D.8.1)

E. Entrepreneurship

By the end of grade 4 students will:
E.4.1 Identify characteristics of an entrepreneur (business owner) (see SS E. 4.12, B.4.1, B.4.3, B.4.7)
E.4.2 Identify reasons for keeping financial records
E.4.3 Explain the cost of theft to business

Business students will:
E.BS.2 Given a business dilemma, identify the problem and analyze possible solutions
E.BS.3 Design a business plan for a specific business
E.BS.6 Prepare financial statements for a planned business

By the end of grade 8 students will:
E.8.2 Recognize opportunities that would lead to a successful business
E.8.5 Explain how supply and demand interact to determine price (see SS D.8.2)
E.8.9 Describe major business activities that occur in any business
E.8.11 Explain the basic operations of a small business

F. Marketing

By the end of grade 4 students will:
F.4.1 Determine product/service preferences of classmates and family members

Business students will:
F.BS.1 Describe and use a marketing plan
F.BS.2 Perform market research
F.BS.3 Test market a product/service
F.BS.4 Analyze the life cycle of a product/service
F.BS.5 Analyze the various factors in pricing for a product/service
F.BS.6 Identify factors that influence the promotional mix of a product/service
F.BS.7 Identify the steps of the selling process
F.BS.8 Develop a distribution plan for a product/service

By the end of grade 8 students will:
F.8.1 Explain the differences between promoting and selling
F.8.2 Contrast different types of promotional campaigns
F.8.3 List factors that influence consumers to buy
F.8.4 Explain the purposes of promotion
F.8.6 Explain how a business identifies products/services needed and wanted by consumers

H. Principles of Management

Business students will:
H.BS.2 Develop short-term strategic plans for a business
H.BS.6 Understand the importance of employer/employee relations

By the end of grade 8 students will:
H.8.2 Describe how to collect and analyze the data in order to make business decisions
H.8.3 Analyze outcomes as a result of business decisions

J. Interpersonal and Leadership Skills

By the end of grade 4 students will:
J.4.7 Describe the advantages of working together as a team
J.4.8 Discuss the importance of being able to work together with people who are different from oneself

Business students will:
J.BS.1 Practice appropriate interpersonal skills in a business setting
J.BS.5 Demonstrate professional behavior in the work environment
J.BS.6 Participate as a member of a team in a business environment

By the end of grade 8 students will:
J.8.2 Demonstrate the ability to work with others
J.8.10 Describe characteristics of a team working together successfully

K. Career Development

By the end of grade 4 students will:
K.4.1 Identify own likes and dislikes and careers that match these preferences
K.4.2 Identify what he/she does well
K.4.3 Identify what he/she needs to improve

Business students will:
K.BS.1 Identify how one's own strengths match skills needed for business career cluster

By the end of grade 8 students will:
K.8.13 Describe appropriate etiquette for work situations

Notes and/or comments about the Business Performance Standards:

English/Language Arts

A. Reading and Literature

By the end of grade 4 students will:
A.4.4 Read to acquire information

- Summarize key details of informational texts, connecting new information to prior knowledge
- Identify a topic of interest and seek information about it by investigating available text resources

B. Writing

By the end of grade 4 students will:
B.4.1 Create or produce writing to communicate with different audiences for a variety of purposes

By the end of grade 8 students will:
B.8.1 Create or produce writing to communicate with different audiences for a variety of purposes

C. Oral Language

By the end of grade 4 students will:
C.4.1 Orally communicate information, opinions, and ideas effectively to different audiences for a variety of purposes
C.4.2 Listen to and comprehend oral communications
C.4.3 Participate effectively in discussion

By the end of grade 8 students will:
C.8.1 Orally communicate information, opinions, and ideas effectively to different audiences for a variety of purposes
C.8.2 Listen to and comprehend oral communications
C.8.3 Participate effectively in discussion

D. Language

By the end of grade 4 students will:
D.4.1 Develop their vocabulary and ability to use words, phrases, idioms, and various grammatical structures as a means of improving communication

By the end of grade 8 students will:
D.8.1 Develop their vocabulary and ability to use words, phrases, idioms, and various grammatical structures as a means of improving communication

E. Media and Technology

By the end of grade 4 students will:
E.4.3 Create media products appropriate to audience and purpose

By the end of grade 8 students will:
E.8.3 Create media products appropriate to audience and purpose

Notes about the English/Language Arts Performance Standards:

Foreign Languages

J. Practical Applications

Elementary, middle, and high school students will:
Jl: Provide service to their school and community through such activities as tutoring, teaching, translating, interpreting, and assisting speakers of other languages

Notes about the Foreign Languages Performance Standards:

Information and Technology Literacy

A. Media and Technology

By the end of grade 4 students will:
A.4.5 Use media and technology to create and present information

By the end of grade 8 students will:
A.8.5 Use media and technology to create and present information

B. Information and Inquiry

By the end of grade 4 students will:
B.4.6 Interpret and use information to solve the problem or answer the question

By the end of grade 8 students will:
B.8.6 Interpret and use information to solve the problem or answer the question

C. Independent Learning

By the end of grade 4 students will:
C.4.1 Pursue information related to various dimensions of personal well being and academic success

By the end of grade 8 students will:
C. 8.1 Pursue information related to various dimensions of personal well being and academic success

D. The Learning Community

By the end of grade 4 students will:
D.4. 1 Participate productively in workgroups or other collaborative learning environments

By the end of grade 8 students will:
D.8.1 Participate productively in workgroups or other collaborative learning environments

Notes about the Information and Technology Literacy Performance Standards:

____

____

____

____

____

Marketing Education

A. Entrepreneurship

By the end of grade 4 students will:
A.4.3 Participate in an entrepreneurial venture; e.g., school-based business (see SS B.4.1, B.4.3, B.4.7, E.4.12)

B. Free Enterprise

By the end of grade 8 students will:
B.8.3 Identify and explain basic economic concepts: supply; demand; production; exchange and consumption; labor, wages, and capital; inflation and deflation; market economy and command economy; and public and private goods and services (see SS D.8.2)

D. Marketing Functions

By the end of grade 4 students will:
D.4.1 Define marketing and the role it plays in our daily lives (see SS D.4.1, D.4.5, D.4.7)
D.4.2 Give examples of the many ways children are consumers (see SS D.4.1, D.4.5, D.4.7)
D.4.3 Illustrate the role of marketing in consumer choice (see SS D.4.1, D.4.2)
D.4.4 Develop a product or service appropriate to a target audience (see LA E.4.3)

By the end of grade 8 students will:
D.8.4 Explain the difference between a buyer and a supplier/vendor

E. Critical Thinking

By the end of grade 4 students will:
E.4.3 Identify a specific problem or concern and evaluate it (see SC C.4.3, C.4.5, C.4.7, H.4.4; M A.4.3; LA F.4.1)

F. Marketing Applications

By the end of grade 4 students will:
F.4.2 Distinguish between businesses that sell products and those that offer services (see SS D.4.5)

By the end of grade 8 students will:
F.8.4 Operate a business or a business simulation as a classroom project (see SS D.12.2, D.12.9)

G. Lifework Development

By the end of grade 8 students will:
G.8.1 Demonstrate how to acquire and use relevant resources to explore choices in education and work (see LA D.8.2; SC G.8.1)

H. Marketing Technology

By the end of grade 4 students will:
H.4.2 Identify uses of technology in business and consumer activities (see SS A.4.9; SC G.4.3, H.4.2)

By the end of grade 8 students will:
H.8.1 Describe uses of technology in consumer and business activities (see LA E.8.1)

Notes about the Marketing Education Performance Standards:

Mathematics

A. Mathematical Process

By the end of grade 4 students will:
A.4.2 Communicate mathematical ideas in a variety of ways, including words, numbers, symbols, pictures, charts, graphs, tables, diagrams, and models

By the end of grade 8 students will:
A.8.1 Uses reasoning abilities to

- Evaluate information
- Perceive patterns
- Identify relationships
- Formulate questions for further exploration
- Evaluate strategies
- Justify statements
- Test reasonableness of results
- Defend work

A.8.4 Develop effective oral and written presentations that include

- appropriate use of technology
- the conventions of mathematical discourse (e.g., symbols, definitions, labeled drawings)

A.8.5 Explain mathematical concepts, procedures, and ideas to others who may not be familiar with them

B. Number Operations and Relations

By the end of grade 4 students will:
B.4.2 Determine the number of things in a set by

- grouping and counting (e.g., by threes, fives, hundreds)
- combining and arranging (e.g., all possible coin combinations amounting to thirty cents)
- estimation, including rounding

By the end of grade 8 students will:
B.8.7 In problem-solving situations, select and use appropriate computational procedures with rational numbers such as

- calculating mentally
- estimating

D. Measurement

By the end of grade 4 students will:
D.4.4 Determine measurements directly by using standard tools to suggested degrees of accuracy

By the end of grade 8 students will:
D.8.3 Determine measurement directly using standard units (metric and US Customary) with theses suggested degrees of accuracy

- lengths to the nearest mm or 1/16 of an inch
- weight (mass) to the nearest 0.1 g or 0.5 ounce

E. Statistics and Probability

By the end of grade 4 students will:
E.4.1 Work with data in the context of real-world situations by

- formulating questions that lead to data collection and analysis
- determining what data to collect and when and how to collect them
- collecting organizing, and displaying data
- drawing reasonable conclusions based on data

By the end of grade 8 students will:
E.8.1 Work with data in the context of real-world situations by

- formulating questions that lead to data collection and analysis
- designing and conducting a statistical investigation
- using technology to generate displays, summarize statistics, and presentations

E.8.2 Organize and display data from statistical investigations using

- appropriate tables, graphs, and/or charts (e.g., circle, bar, or line for multiple sets of data)
- appropriate plots (e.g., line, stem-and-leaf; box, scatter)

F. Algebraic Relationships

By the end of grade 8 students will:
F.8.2 Work with linear and nonlinear patterns and relationships in a variety of ways, including

- representing them with tables, with graphs, and with algebraic expressions, equations, and inequalities
- describing and interpreting their graphical representations (e.g., slope, rate of change, intercepts) using them as models of real-world phenomena
- describing a real-world phenomenon that a given graph might represent

Notes about the Mathematics Performance Standards:

Music

Composition

By the end of grade 4 students in general music class will:
Dl: Create and arrange music to accompany readings and dramatizations

Notes about the Music Performance Standards:

Personal Financial Literacy

A. Relating Income and Education

By the end of grade 4 students will:
A.1 Understand how career choice, education, skills, entrepreneurship, and economic conditions affect income.
A.4.1.1 Be aware of how career choices, education choices, and skills affect income.
A.4.1.2 Recognize the difference between a job and a career.
A.2 Understand the sources of income and alternative resources.
A.4.2.1 Identify potential sources of income.
A.4.2.2 Identify various employee employment benefits.
A.3 Explain how income affects lifestyle choices and spending decisions.
A.4.3.1 Explain how income affects spending.
A.4.3.2 Determine how personal interest and talents can affect career choice.
A.4 Explain how taxes and employee benefits relate to disposable income.
A.4.1.1 Explain the meaning and purposes of taxes.

By the end of grade 8 students will:
A.1 Understand how career choice, education, skills, entrepreneurship, and economic conditions affect income.
A.8.1.1 Relate how career choices, education choices, skill, entrepreneurship, and economic conditions affect income
A.8.1.2 Describe the unique characteristics of both a job and a career.
A.2 Understand the sources of income and alternative resources.
A.8.2.1 Identify and understand factors affecting income.
A.8.2.2 Understand how employee benefits relate to income.
A.3 Explain how income affects lifestyle choices and spending decisions.
A.8.3.1 Examine how income affects choices and spending decisions
A.8.3.2 Investigate how individual skills and abilities can be applied to a career choice.
A.4 Explain how taxes and employee benefits relate to disposable income.
A.8.4.1 Discuss concepts associated with taxes and income.

B. Money Management

By the end of grade 4 students will:
B.1 Demonstrate ability to use money management skills and strategies.
B.4.1.1 Identify the consequences of various financial decisions related to spending and saving.
B.4.1.2 Define a budget and its importance.
B.2 Understand the purposes and services of financial institutions.
B.4.2.1 Identify the purposes of financial institutions in the community.
B.4.2.2 Understand the difference between cash, check, credit card, and debit card.
B.3 Develop a financial vision based on an examination of personal values.
B.4.3.1 Identify ways to earn and save for a future event.
B.4.3.2 Recognize age-appropriate financial goals.
B.4. Understand the history, purposes, roles, and responsibilities related to taxation
B.4.4.2 Explain how taxes are collected and used

By the end of grade 8 students will:
B.1 Demonstrate ability to use money management skills and strategies.
B.8.1.1 Formulate and compare money management choices that enable individuals to progress toward stated financial goals.
B.8.1.2 Prepare a budget for various applications(personal, family, business)
B.2 Understand the purposes and services of financial institutions.
B.8.2.1 Analyze and select appropriate financial institutions to assist with meeting various personal financial needs and goals.
B.8.2.2 Describe various financial products or services(ATM, debit cards, credit cards, checkbooks, etc.) and the most appropriate use of each.
B.3 Develop a financial vision based on an examination of personal values.
B.8.3.1 Develop a plan to secure funding for a future event.
B.8.3.2 Analyze and discuss the long-range impact of setting personal financial goals.

C. Credit and Debt Management

By the end of grade 4 students will:
C.1 Identify and evaluate credit products and services.
C.4.4.1 Explain the difference between products and services.
C.4.1.2 Describe the concept of a loan.
C.2 Identify and compare sources of credit
C.4.2.1 Describe the difference between credit and debt.
C.3 Identify and evaluate interest rates, fees, and other charges.
C.4.3.2 Understand the relationship between income and expenses
C.7 Understand how to leverage debt.
C.4.7.1 List reasons why people borrow.

By the end of grade 8 students will:
C.1 Identify and evaluate credit products and services.
C.8.1.1 Compare the benefits and costs of spending decisions.
C.8.1.2 Analyze information about products and services.
C.2 Identify and compare sources of credit.
C.8.2.3 Explain credit terminology
C.3 Identify and evaluate interest rates, fees, and other charges.
C.8.3.1 Explain options for payment on credit cards.
C.7 Understand how to leverage debt.
C.8.7.1 List the purposes of debt.
C.8 Describe the implications of bankruptcy.
C.8.8.2 Examine ways to avoid bankruptcy.

D. Planning, Savings, and Investing

By the end of grade 4 students will:
D.1. Apply strategies for creating wealth/building assets.
D.4.1.1 Explain the principle of savings.
D.2 Match appropriate financial services and products with specified goals.
D.4.2.1 Identify various ways to save.
D.3 Describe and relationships between saving and investing.
D.4.3.1 Define investing.
D.4.3.2 Differentiate between saving and investing.
D.5 Demonstrate ability to use decision-making processes in making financial decisions related to planning, saving, and investing.
D.4.5.1 Describe reasons to save.

By the end of grade 8 students will:
D.1 Apply strategies for creating wealth/building assets.
D.8.1.3 Define the difference between income and wealth.
D.3 Describe and relationships between saving and investing.
D.8.3.2 Describe reasons for saving, reasons for investing, and entrepreneurship.

E. Becoming A Critical Consumer

By the end of grade 4 students will:
E.1 Understand the impact of contextual factors associated with consumer decision making.
E.4.1.1 Identify factors to consider when making one's own consumer decisions
E.6 Examine critically the impact of socio-cultural norms and demographics related to money, saving, and spending
E.4.6.2 Identify the benefits and costs of buying goods.
E.4.6.3 Identify elements of being a responsible consumer.

By the end of grade 8 students will:
E.1 Understand the impact of contextual factors associated with consumer decision making.
E.8.1.1 Examine individual differences in decisions made as a consumer.
E.2 Investigate the purposes, strategies, and effects of various business practices, including sales schemes or scams
E.8.2.1 Compare and contrast advertising for opinion vs. fact
E.8.2.2 Examine the impact of selected business practices.
E.5 Identify sources of consumer protection and assistance including public institutions and private organizations
E.8.5.2 Identify resources that can be used in making consumer decisions.
E.6 Examine critically the impact of socio-cultural norms and demographics related to money, saving, and spending, and so forth.
E.8.6.3 Compare the value of goods or services from different sellers.
E.8.6.3 Demonstrate aspects of being a responsible consumer.

F. Community and Financial Responsibility

By the end of grade 4 students will:
F.1 Understand factors that affect citizen financial decisions and actions
F.4.1.2 Recognize attitudes, assumptions, and patterns of behavior regarding money, saving, investing, and work.
F.2 Practice skills related to fiscal responsibility and personal decision making.
F.4.2.1 Identify processes for responsible financial planning and decision making.

By the end of grade 8 students will:
F.1 Understand factors that affect citizen financial decisions and actions
F.8.1.2 Analyze attitudes, assumptions, and patterns of behavior regarding money, saving, investing, and work.

G. Risk Management

By the end of grade 4 students will:
G.1 Understand the nature of personal financial risk and the importance of protecting against financial loss
G.4.1.1 Define financial risk.

By the end of grade 8 students will:
G.1 Understand the nature of personal financial risk and the importance of protecting against financial loss
G.8.1.3 Identify ways to manage the possibility of financial loss

Notes about the Personal Financial Literacy Performance Standards:

Science

G. Science Applications

By the end of grade 4 students will:
G.4.1 Identity the technology used by someone employed in a job or position in Wisconsin and explain how the technology helps

Notes about the Science Performance Standards:

Social Studies

D. Economics: Production, Distribution, Exchange, and Consumption

By the end of grade 4 students will:
D.4.1 Describe and explain the role of money, banking, and saving in everyday life

E. The Behavioral Sciences: Individuals, Institutions, and Society
By the end of grade 4 students will:
E.4.10 Give examples and explain how the media may influence opinions, choices, and decisions

Notes about the Social Studies Performance Standards:

Technology Education

C. Human Ingenuity

By the end of grade 4 students will:
C.4.4 Explain why people work collaboratively to design and produce products

Notes about the Technology Education Performance Standards:

Theatre

F. Theatre Production

By the end of grade 4 students will:
E4: Create publicity for a dramatic presentation

Notes about the Theatre Performance Standards:

Visual Arts

E. Visual Communication and Expression

By the end of grade 4 students will:
E4. Communicate basic ideas by producing visual communication forms useful in everyday life, such as sketches, diagrams, graphs, plans, and models

Notes about the Visual Arts Performance Standards:

SECTION 3

BUSINESS AND EDUCATION PARTNERSHIPS

INTRODUCTION

A school store or school based business is an excellent opportunity for you, your students, or the school to form partnerships with local or regional businesses. With a little networking and communication, the business and education partnerships are endless.

Business and education partnerships are defined as formal cooperative relationships between school districts and businesses that benefit and involve pupils, professional staff businesses, and the larger community. Partnerships promote better education, develop a better-trained work force, and strengthen the system by improving communication and understanding between schools and communities. The connections between growth, employability skills, and productivity are essential. Together schools and businesses can ensure that students are adequately prepared for the jobs of the future.

PARTNERSHIP QUOTES

The following quotes about business and education partnerships are a bit dated. Today's research parallels this research, but I think the following research is worded better and can be applied and characterized in today's business and education partnerships.

"Education has a direct impact on employment, productivity, and the nation's ability to compete in world markets. Economically, it's in the best interest of our businesses to have our schools do the job of preparing our youth well. However, businesses nationwide have found young people ill prepared to function in the increasingly technological world. As a result, businesses have committed significant resources to employee training. It is estimated that training, not formal education, provides the skills for two out of three jobs and that corporate training is a larger system than the entire elementary, secondary, and higher education systems put together." Anthony P. Carnevale, "The Learning Enterprise," Training and Development Journal 40.1, January 1986, p. 18.

"Partnerships should be designed so that no single member provides all the assistance. The secret is to spread the workload so that many persons make some contributions. While this approach takes more time and coordination, it ensures closer collaboration." Anita G Garber, The Nuts and Bolts of Business/Education Partnerships, Enterprise, April 1984, p. 13.

"Partnerships must go beyond corporations donating money; businesses need to be involved at the curriculum level by donating their time and expertise. Business leaders typically find they get as much as they give to partnership ventures. They often find working with young people a satisfying experience. Schools can help business understand the complexities involved in educating youth, and that they need the help of the business community in bringing relevancy to course content. Schools also need business help to ensure that students are employable, since it's business that provides future jobs." Anthony P. Carnevale, The Learning Enterprise, Training and Development Journal 40.1, January 1986, p. 18.

COMPONENTS OF BUSINESS AND EDUCATION PARTNERSHIPS

- An advisory council of local business representatives, community leaders, and school personnel is responsible for creating and maintaining partnerships
- Staff development activities are designed to enhance the awareness of school staff and teachers about the needs, methods, and means for integrating the business/education partnership concept into all phases of curriculum; to bring private industry personnel into the schools so they can better understand what the schools do; and to provide individual teachers with private/public sector job site experiences
- Resources, both equipment and personnel, are shared so that each partner benefits
- Planning, implementation, finding, and evaluation of projects, programs, and services are conducted cooperatively and collaboratively, and are based on measurable and agreed upon objectives
- Partnership activities enhance economic development and job retention/creation in the local labor market
- Partnership activities further school improvement and educational reform

PARTNERSHIP EXAMPLES AND PROJECTS

- Work experience
- Job shadowing
- Career fairs
- Plant and office tours
- Work simulation
- Equipment loan, donation, or purchase
- Business speakers
- Adopt-a-school program
- Advisory committees with business representatives
- Career exploration programs
- Co-op programs
- Fieldtrips
- Job-seeking skill information
- Job-keeping information
- Classroom instruction by business people
- Job counseling in the field
- Education liaison department
- School staff on business development committees
- Teachers working in business, industry, or government [summer internships]
- Teachers providing services and expertise for business or industry

OPPORTUNITIES FROM PARTNERSHIPS

- Share knowledge
- Enhance the understanding of roles and abilities
- Use factories and workplaces as classrooms
- Provide teachers with business work experience
- Share and exchange human resources—help to solve administrative problems
- Improve student understanding of business roles
- Provide part-time employment (internships, on-the-job training) for students
- Sponsor continuing education programs for teachers
- Fund grants for curriculum development
- Serve on curriculum advisory committees
- Develop a work force pool through job oriented classes
- Develop an awareness of opportunities for females, minorities, and economically disadvantaged students
- Develop realistic experimental exercises at the elementary and middle school level
- Provide needs assessment seminars related to business and education
- Provide technology seminars
- Provide tax incentives for businesses to develop partnerships
- Use schools for retraining business employees
- Support student organizations
- Support business and education partnership programs such as inventorships, business worlds (locally), cooperative education, and adopt-a-school or adopt-a-class programs

SAMPLE PARTNERSHIPS

- A bank working with an elementary classroom to set up a bank simulation unit
- An "adopt-a-school" program in which a business works with schools on curriculum, placement, public relations, and resources to enhance attitudes, skills, and knowledge necessary for success in the specific business fields
- A radio or television station providing equipment, experience, and curriculum in media
- Cash awards for teachers judged to be excellent in providing skills to students
- Paid internships for students to learn the operation of a business
- A newspaper providing journalistic opportunities, and speakers for career roundtables
- Business sponsored essays or poster contests stressing business needs and concerns

Providing professional development or a salary for teachers to implement business • specific curriculum

- Using community business equipment to print or reproduce school newspapers or documents
- Businesses donating space and equipment for science fairs or other activities
- Cooperative development of a nature park, or arboretum, on company or school land
- Law firms supporting instruction in judicial proceedings, helping with mock courts, and coordinating court visits
- Art students and/or teachers assisting in logo development for a small business

- Business and/or English teachers and/or classes assisting in writing or editing manuals for businesses

ADOPT-A-SCHOOL/CLASS PROGRAM

Schools and/or teachers participating in a business and education partnership can ask a local business owner or business representative to "adopt their school/class" for a period of time. Throughout that time, students will focus on the type of business represented by the adopting business and how it contributes to the quality of life in the community and throughout the world. Classroom instruction can be connected to "the world of work" through direct contact with business employees and with business and manufacturing environments. Activities and depth of study will depend on the age of the students, business complexity, and goals of your school.

The following is reprinted/excerpted from Mentoring Youth for Success with permission from The Wisconsin Department of Public Instruction, 125 South Webster Street, Madison, WI 53702; 800/243-8782.

Objectives for Adopt-A-School/Class Program

- Provide students in grades K-Adult with exposure to local and regional businesses
- Strengthen the partnership between schools and businesses in the community
- Expand student awareness of occupational opportunities in their community
- Expand student awareness of services and manufacturing worldwide
- Demonstrate the importance of education to occupational choices and success

Suggested Conditions for Adopt-A-School/Class Program

- Adoption is for one academic year
- Adoption match based on complexity or nature of business and comprehension of students
- Establish a minimum number of contacts per year between class and business
- Conduct an orientation and planning sequence between teacher and business representatives prior to the onset of adoption

Activity Ideas for Adopt-A-School/Class Program

- Informational interviews with local businesses and industry to determine skills needed for employment
- Arrange field trips to tour adopting businesses
- Conduct field trips to tour similar businesses to see how size or technical differences change manufacturing methods, management approaches, occupational opportunities, etc.
- Arrange classroom visits by business representatives to explain operations, products, occupations, customers, etc.
- Conduct joint business ventures
- Explore occupations through job shadowing
- Ongoing communications between business employees and students (face-to-face, business memos, business letters, fax, e-mail, internet)

- Presentations by students to business employees to explain skills they are learning that would help them function in occupations available through business
- Charting/graphing of production, personnel use, etc.
- Create a business profile reference for each adopting business for other classes to reference
- Have students choose a business and solicit the adoption by written proposal or scheduled meeting
- Classroom visits by entrepreneurs to discuss entrepreneurship as a viable career option
- Interest inventories and classroom discussions of their importance in planning educational and career goals
- Annual thank-you banquet attended by students and business owners/employees
- Periodically invite someone from the community to work at the school store to provide interaction with students thereby gaining insight into the school store and/or other entrepreneurship education programs

MENTORING PROGRAM (Find a retired or current business person to act as a mentor to students)

The role of the mentor could include:

- Plan the sequence of work skills to be learned by the student(s), in cooperation with local school instructors
- Regularly evaluate the progress of learning at the workplace
- Show the student how work tasks are done and explain why they are important
- Help the student avoid problems and errors on work assignments
- Provide support, encouragement, and direction
- Help build the self-confidence and self-esteem of the student
- Be alert to personal problems that may interfere with school or work and seek help from appropriate sources for the student
- Meet with the student's parents or guardians and school personnel at least once every grading period to report on the student's progress
- Communicate regularly with the school liaison and/or the designated program coordinator to discuss any problems and to ensure that work-based learning experiences and classroom instruction are integrated

All mentoring programs should be carefully planned, monitored, and tailored to meet the specific needs of students. Program coordinators are encouraged to arrange periodic meetings of all mentors. These meetings can provide an opportunity to share experiences and information about the mentoring program, and can provide training on working with and supervising adolescents.

JOB SHADOWING

What is job shadowing?
Job shadowing is an opportunity for students to explore the world of work by "shadowing," at an area company. They should tour, observe, ask questions and come to understand what a particular job or industry is really like.

Can anyone imagine a better way for students to learn about an occupation that interests them? What will students learn?
Among the things that they will learn are:

- What skills, talents, and qualifications are needed on the job?
- What advantages and drawbacks does a particular job have?
- How will the skills you're learning in school right now be used on the job?
- What kind of work setting will you find yourself in if you selected a career in the field you're interested in?

What do students need to do to arrange to job shadow?
They will need to start by contacting their guidance counselor or appropriate facilitator and express their interest in job shadowing. He or she will tell them exactly what the process is. Students will need to:

- Do some research about their career interest
- Make sure they have turned in the appropriate permission slips, forms, etc
- Prepare a list of questions to take along on their shadowing trip
- Dress appropriately for their visit (neat, clean, school clothes are appropriate)
- Thank the business person they visited when they leave and send a short thank you note after their visit
- Let their guidance counselor or facilitator know how the visit went and what they learned

Things To Remember When Shadowing

- You're there to learn, be sure to ask questions of your host
- Request permission before approaching other people at the work site
- You may be near equipment so don't touch anything. Follow all safety rules and stay close to your host

Questions Students Can Ask When Job Shadowing

What does your company do?
What skills are needed to do your job?
Did your company train you?
How did your education prepare you for this job?
How did you get this job?
What are the future job opportunities with your company?
When is your job most exciting to you?
When is your job most boring?
What is a typical day on the job like?
When and how did you decide on this career?
What should a student do to get a job like yours?
How many job openings will there be in your occupation in the future?

SECTION 4

FINANCIAL LITERACY

INTRODUCTION

The financial literacy section of this book was created and implemented when I taught in elementary and junior high. The students loved it. They were excited and motivated because it opened their eyes to authentic hands-on learning that connected school work with career work/awareness, and the math associated with real-life living. This section, "turns on the light bulb," to the real-world process of establishing a monthly budget and being a consumer. Students experience actual things they are going to encounter soon in their lives.

This section is a holistic conclusion to being employed, like the students are at the school store. Just think about it. What happens in real life after someone is finished with their educational venture of high school, technical college, apprenticeship, or college? They usually get a job or start a small business. Either way, they seek employment. Once employed, they start the process of establishing a monthly budget, finding a place to live, and becoming a consumer using their own finances. That is exactly what this section of the book is about. It addresses the process of living by incorporating many of the things that happen in real life.

The first two activity topics called "Calculating Earnings" and "Calculating Monthly Net Income" set the stage for establishing a monthly budget. In the "Calculating Earnings" activity, the students find an occupation and establish a yearly income. The second activity "Calculating Monthly Net Income," has the students pay taxes and determine exactly how much money they will have to work with for a month.

In the financial literacy section, there are many options and opportunities to do some math, do some career exploration, do some financial decision making, and build life-long skills. It all depends on your mission and goals, the time available, and the age of your students.

The versatility of these activities makes them modifiable for a variety of ages. The different activities and math problems can be adjusted to meet the needs of your students. The concepts in this section can also be adjusted accordingly.

Each activity has example problems of the topic, followed by student practice problems (problems the students can calculate), followed by hands-on student activities (real-life activities of becoming a consumer).

- ***The answers to all the 'Student Practice Problems' can be found at the end of the financial literacy section.***

- ***The examples of sales tax, interest rates, pricing, gas rates, and insurance rates in Section 4 are examples. Please feel free to adjust these amounts and any other pricing amounts to any number you feel may be more relevant to your region or state.***

CALCULATING EARNINGS

Introduction

In the Calculating Earnings activity, the students begin thinking about their occupations in relation to their income. The students begin the activity by reviewing three examples called, "Example Problems: Calculating Earnings." These three examples are examples of different people working different jobs and experiencing different ways to earn an income. There is an example of regular time wages, overtime wages, and commissioned wages. It gives the students some possible job ideas and examples of wages and income. These examples are real-life situations that many people encounter when determining their career vs. income and income vs. career.

After the students review the three example problems, their next task is to do some practice problems of their own. The practice problems are called, "Student Practice Problems: Calculating Earnings."

After the students do their practice problems, their next task is called "Hands-On Student Activity: Choose Your Occupation and Establish a Yearly Income." This task is where students find an occupation and establish a yearly income.

The student's occupation decisions can be based on many different scenarios, depending on your scope and goals. Ideally, the student's occupation could be a small business owner because that is what they just developed and operated earlier; a school based business (school store). Their income, after paying all business expenses, could be say $30,000.00, or whatever you feel is relevant. However, since this book also focuses on career exploration and decision making, the consumer math section gives the students the option to choose a different occupation besides being a small business owner. It is the flexibility of the consumer math section that allows students to fill out the "Hands-On Student Activity: Choose Your Occupation and Establish a Yearly Income" activity with any occupation they choose.

There are many ways for students to research, evaluate, and choose an occupation. One scenario may be that you take the students to the library and research occupations, salaries, and various employment opportunities. The research can come from videos, computers, the classified sections of the newspapers, books, magazines, or job linked websites. Another scenario can be where the students take an occupation that the school store incorporates. The school store has different positions with different income potentials. For example, advertising associate, bookkeeping associate, buying associate, inventory associate, sales associate, and managing associate are just a few. A third scenario could be where all the students pick the same occupation so that everyone has the same income and profession. A fourth scenario is that the students can take the "occupation activity" home and brainstorm with their parents about an occupation, or even take their parent's occupation. A fifth scenario could be to put on an occupation/job clinic with local businesses in the community.

For younger students, you may just want to have them choose a "fun" occupation and estimate the yearly income, within reason. For example, choosing a professional football player making three million a year would not be feasible to this activity.

It is the yearly gross income, from the student's occupational choice, that is needed for the rest of the consumer math project to unfold.

Example Problems: Calculating Earnings

Example 1:

Bill earns $12.00 an hour as a carpenter. He works 38 hours a week.

A. How much does he earn in a week?
Answer: $12.00 X 38 = $456.00

B. How much does he earn in a year (hint: 52 weeks in a year)?
Answer: $456.00 X 52 = $23,712.00

Example 2:

Pattie earns $8.00 per hour as a clerk. She works 45 hours a week. She gets paid overtime (time and a half) for all hours over 40.

A. How much does she get paid per week?
Answer: Regular time: $8.00 x 40 = $320.00
Overtime: $8.00 x 1.5 = $12.00 an hour
$12.00 x 5 = $60.00 overtime pay
Total per week is $320 regular pay + $60 overtime pay = $380.00

B. How much does she earn in a year?
Answer: Total per year is $380 x 52 = $19,760.00

Example 3:

Kayla works in a jewelry store. She is paid $1000 a month plus a 2% commission on all she sells. In a month she sells $15,000 worth of jewelry.

A. What does she earn in a month?
Answer: 2% as a decimal is .02
.02 x $15,000 = $300.00
In one month she makes $1000 + $300 = $1300.00

B. What does she earn in a year?
Answer: In one year she makes 12 x $1300 = $15,600.00

Student Practice Problems: Calculating Earnings

1. Tim makes $7.75 an hour at McDonald's as a cashier. He works 32 hours a week.

   A. How much does he earn in a week?

   B. How much does he earn in a year?

2. Jose makes $12.00 an hour working at Banta Corporation. He works 35 hours a week.

   A. How much will he make in a week?

   B. How much will he make in a year?

3. Beyonce works two jobs. She earns $7.75 an hour as a hotel cleaner. She works 30 hours a week at the Hilton. Beyonce also works as a model on weekends. Here she earns $13.00 an hour for 8 hours work.

   A. How much does she make in a week?

   B. How much does she make in a year?

4. Dakota works 52 hours a week building houses. He gets $13.00 per hour. He also gets time and a half for any hours over 40.

   A. How much will he make in a week?

   B. How much does he make in a year?

5. Ming is a secretary. She makes $11.00 an hour. She works 55 hours a week. She gets paid time and a half for all hours over 40 hours.

   A. What does she make a week?

   B. What does she make a year?

6. Marshall earns $20.00 an hour working on building saunas. He works 12 hours each weekend. He also has a weekday job that pays $650 a week.

   A. What is his total pay per week?

   B. What is his total pay per year?

7. Tanya sells stereo equipment. She makes $1200 a month plus 5% of what she sells. She sells about $8000 worth of equipment a month.

   A. What does she make in a month?

   B. What does she make in a year?

8. Louis is in real estate. He makes a 6% commission on all his sales. He sold 7 houses worth a total of $556,000 in a year.

   A. What did he earn last year?

Hands-On Student Activity: Choose Your Occupation and Establish a Yearly Gross Income

Occupation Name______________________________________

Description of Job____________________________________

Approximately how much do you make per year before taxes (Yearly Gross Income)?______________________

What are your duties and responsibilities?

____

____

____

____

Do you perform a service? If yes, what service?

____

Do you make a product? If yes, what product or products?

____

Is it hard to get a job in this field? Yes or no and why?

____

What are the aspects of the job you enjoy?

____

What are the aspects of the job you don't enjoy?

____

What type of education do you think you need for your job (High School, Apprenticeship, Technical School, Four Year College, More than four years of college)?________________

____

CALCULATING MONTHLY NET INCOME

Introduction

After the students have determined their occupation and yearly income, it is time to pay taxes so they know how much money they have to work with. The student's yearly gross incomes from their occupational choice, and their monthly net income, are two different things.

There are three main taxes that come out of a gross paycheck (total check before taxes). The first is state tax. The second is federal tax. The third is F.I.C.A. tax. FICA tax is the Federal Insurance Contribution Act. Basically, it's a federal act dealing with the tax paid towards Social Security and Medicare. There are other taxes, dues, and contributions that come out of a paycheck, but we are only going to incorporate these three main taxes to keep this concept easier to understand.

Depending on your scope and goals, you can make the tax portion of the consumer math section as inclusive or as simple as you want. The most inclusive way would be to supply a copy of the state and federal tax forms to the students. The students can use their data interpretation skills to look up their tax increment and see what the state and federal taxes would be for a single person and just subtract those amounts from their gross income. Then, calculate FICA tax (6% of gross income) and subtract that also. After the students subtract state tax, federal tax, and FICA tax from the yearly gross income, the amount left over is the yearly net income. Next, the students just have to take the yearly net income, and divide by twelve to get the monthly net income. This is the number to use when creating this monthly budget.

The easiest way to calculate state, federal, and FICA tax for a single person is to just multiply the yearly gross income by about 25% or .25 (state = 5.7%, federal = 13.5%, FICA = 6%, approximately; you can use whatever percentages you feel are relevant to your state). Then, deduct that total from the yearly gross income to get the yearly net income (take home pay). After that, divide the yearly net income by 12 to get the monthly net income. This is the number to use when creating this monthly budget.

For students that may have difficulty doing the math, those students could just be assigned a monthly net income such as $1000 per month, $1300 per month, or whatever you think is reasonable. Getting the exact deductions and doing the exact math may not be as important as the concept of a "monthly net income". It depends on your goals, and the age of your students.

Example Problems: Calculating Monthly Net Income

The following are two examples for calculating monthly net income. Example 1 is calculated using the Federal and State 2010 tax tables for a single person. Example 2 is done using the estimate of a 25% deduction that includes the Federal, State, and FICA taxes.

<u>Example 1:</u>

Occupation: Teacher

Marital Status: Single

Total Yearly Income: $28,500.00

Read the Federal and State tax from the tax chart to locate amount of tax to pay.

Federal Tax: $3861.00

State Tax: $1626.00

FICA tax is 6% of total yearly income. So $28,500 x .06 = $1710.00

Total Tax = $7197.00 (State + Federal + FICA)

Yearly Net Income = $21,303.00 (Total Yearly Income—Total Tax)

Monthly Net Income = $1775.25 (Yearly Net Income divided by 12)

<u>Example 2</u>

Occupation: Teacher

Marital Status: Single

Total Yearly Income: $28,500.00

Total Tax: $7125.00 (Total Yearly Income x .25)

Yearly Net Income: $21,375.00 (Total Yearly Income—Total Tax)

Monthly Net Income: $1781.25 (Yearly Net Income divided by 12)

As you can see, example 1 and example 2 have very close monthly net incomes. The difference is so small that it won't make a big difference. So, choose which method is appropriate for you and your students.

Student Practice Problems: Calculating Monthly Net Income

The following problems can be done using a federal tax table, a state tax table, and 6% for FICA tax, or by simply deducting 25% of your gross pay.

Problem 1:

Occupation: Plumber
Marital Status: Single
Total Yearly Income: $42,000.00

Calculate:

A. Federal tax____________
B. State tax______________
C. FICA tax (6% of Total Yearly Income)_______________
D. Total Tax__________________
E. Yearly Net Income_____________
F. Monthly Net Income___________

————or————

Calculate:

A. Total Tax (25% of Total Yearly Income)__________
B. Yearly Net Income____________________
C. Monthly Net Income___________________

Problem 2:

Occupation: Social Worker
Marital Status: Single
Total Yearly Income: $29,000.00

Calculate:

A. Federal tax____________
B. State tax______________
C. FICA tax (6% of Total Yearly Income)_______________
D. Total Tax_____________________
E. Total Net Income_______________
F. Monthly Net Income____________

————or————

Calculate:

A. Total Tax (25% of Total Yearly Income)_______________
B. Yearly Net Income________________
C. Monthly Net Income________________

Problem 3:

Occupation: Cashier
Marital Status: Single
Total Yearly Income: $18,360.00

Calculate:

A. Federal tax____________
B. State tax______________
C. FICA tax (6% of Total Yearly Income)_______________
D. Total Tax____________________
E. Total Net Income______________
F. Monthly Net Income_____________

————or————

Calculate:

A. Total Tax (25% of yearly pay)_________________
B. Yearly Net Pay_______________
C. Monthly Net Pay_________________

Hands-On Student Activity: Calculate Your Monthly Net Income
(Your marital status is single)

Occupation________________________

Total Yearly Income____________________

Calculate:

Federal Tax (from current tax table)________________________

State Tax (from current tax table)__________________________

FICA Tax (6% of Total Yearly Income)________________________

Total Tax__________________________

Yearly Net Income_____________________

Monthly Net Income____________________

————or————

Occupation________________________

Total Yearly Income____________________

Calculate:

Total Tax (Yearly Income x .25)__________

Yearly Net Income_____________________

Monthly Net Income____________________

The monthly net income is the amount to use when starting your monthly budget. This is the amount of money you have to work with to pay bills for the month. You do not want your expenses for the month to be more than your monthly net income. The amount you just calculated will be your beginning balance in your checkbook to pay bills for the month. There will be no credit card use or borrowing money to pay bills.

Describe what you have learned from calculating your monthly net income for your occupation.

____

____

____

____

____

GETTING STARTED WITH A MONTHLY BUDGET

Introduction

The next four pages give students a monthly budget organizer, a checkbook example, a student checkbook, and some blank checks.

The monthly budget organizer is a list of the majority of the monthly expenses that most people regularly have. The organizer is there to help students see, at a glance, possible monthly expenses. Some of the expenses may not be used, while other expenses may need to be created. There are a couple of places at the bottom of the organizer (other) in case there are other monthly expenses not listed that you would like to incorporate.

The checkbook example is a sample to show students the process of sustaining a checkbook. The beginning balance of $1781.25 is the monthly net income from the previous tax example of a single teacher making $28,500.00 per year. As checks get written out for bills, the check amount gets deducted from the previous balance.

The checkbook example is missing some areas that a normal checkbook has (credit/debit columns, etc.). This was done to keep the checkbook maintenance simple. This is only a budget for one month so all we need is a beginning balance. The students aren't getting paid every week or two. Therefore, every entry is subtracted from the previous balance as checks are written. The checkbook process can be modified according to your needs.

The student checkbook is the checkbook the students will use to do their monthly transactions. Similar to the checkbook example, after the students enter their beginning monthly balance, they will subtract their expenses as the expenses become known. The check number, the date, and who the check is to will also be similar. The students enter their monthly net income from the previous "Hands-On Student Activity: Calculate Your Monthly Net Income" activity for their beginning monthly balance. That amount is the only money they will have to use for their month of bills.

The checks page is the place where students can practice writing checks. After the checks are written, the amounts are deducted in the student checkbook. More checks may need to be made, depending on your goals. You may want a check written for every expense, so that the students have practice writing the numbers in words and visa versa.

Depending on your scope and goals, you may want to talk about the need of opening a checking account, ordering checks, and other concepts related to having a checking account. For junior high students who may be getting a part-time job soon, talking about the process of establishing a checking account may be a viable option. Other options include taking a field trip to a bank or having someone from a local bank come in and talk to the class about banking questions. This is another good opportunity to form a business and education partnership.

Monthly Budget Organizer

Category	Monthly Budget Notes	Payment
Rent		
Rent Insurance		
Heat		
Water		
Electricity		
Phone		
Cable		
Internet		
Clothing		
Food		
Car		
Car Insurance		
Gas/Oil		
Recreation		
Savings (optional)		
Other		
Other		
Other		

Checkbook Example

Note: This checkbook is a simplified version of a real checkbook. It has been simplified to the entries that are needed most. As you can see, a beginning balance is entered. From there, as checks are written out, the check number, date, who the payment is to, and the amount of the checks are documented in the checkbook. Then, the check amount is subtracted from the previous balance.

Check Number	Date	To:	Balance
			Enter beginning balance in the box below
			1781.25
1.	2/1	Landlord	-575.00
			1206.25
2.	2/3	Phone Provider	-57.63
			1148.62
3.	2/5	Heat and/or Electric Provider	-149.27
			999.35
4.	2/10	Water Provider	-59.99
			939.36
		ETC.	

Student Checkbook

Check Number	Date	To:	Balance
			Enter beginning balance in the box below
1.			
2.			

Blank Checks

Your Name
Your Street
Your Town, State 08080

Check Number________
________ 20________

Pay to the order of________________________________ $

____Dollars

YOUR BANK
Your Town, State

SAMPLE VOID

Memo____________________

____
Signature

:000067894 : 12345678

Your Name
Your Street
Your Town, State 08080

Check Number________
________ 20________

Pay to the order of________________________________ $

____Dollars

YOUR BANK
Your Town, State

SAMPLE VOID

Memo____________________

____
Signature

:000067894 : 12345678

CALCULATING MONTHLY BUDGET EXPENSES

This part of Section 4 begins the process of having the students become consumers and acquiring monthly expenses. There are many different and unique monthly expenses that people encounter. Even though monthly expenses are vast and varied, there are some common monthly expenses the majority of people encounter. Rent, phone, TV, internet, auto, clothing, appliance, and food are the common expenses I think the majority of people encounter.

Knowing this, I would like to think that people try to live "within" their own unique budget. That is the goal.

These expenses can be modified depending on your scope, goals, and age of your students.

Rental and Other Related Expenses

Figure 4-1

Introduction

The first, and probably one of the biggest expenses of a monthly budget, is rental costs. Rental costs can vary from city to city and state to state. Depending on your scope and goals for this project, the rental expenses can be made as holistic and real-life as possible or the rental expenses can be made more simplistic (an estimate). Figure 4-1 shows an example of advertising for apartments.

Calculating the monthly rental expense can be as holistic or as simple as you want. For a more holistic approach, let's first consider the real-life rental process for most individuals. When finding a place to rent, most people research different options in the newspaper, on-line, in catalogs, on bulletin boards, word of mouth, etc. Once they find a place they may like, they set up an appointment to go see the place. If they like it, they sign a lease. If not, they continue their search until a suitable place is found. Depending on your time and objectives, it would be most appropriate to simulate that process. I found bringing in newspapers and catalogs creates the most excitement. For example, when I did this part of the consumer math project, I had the students do some research for a place to rent. I brought in local newspapers, catalogs, and anything else I could get my hands on to give the students different options to choose from and find a place to rent. Also, I had one rule when finding a place to rent. The rule is that the students could have as many people living in the apartment as they want, but each student needed their own bedroom. Two people needed a two bedroom apartment; three people needed a three bedroom apartment, and so on.

The easiest way to calculate rental costs is to estimate. One way to estimate rental costs is to take your monthly net income and divide by three. For example, if a student's monthly net income is $1500, then $1500 divided by three is $500 a month for rent. Of course, that amount can be adjusted accordingly to whatever you think is reasonable. The concept of rental expenses is more important than the exact amount.

There are other costs involved in "putting a roof over your head." These things include heat, water, and electricity. Sometimes, there are one or more utilities included in the rent. Sometimes, there are no utilities included in the rent. If the student's rent includes any of these three utilities, then the student does not have to put those expenses in the monthly budget organizer and write out checks for them. If those utilities are not included in the rent, then estimate that heat will be approximately $70 per month average, water will be $40 per month average, and electricity will be $55 per month average. These estimates can be adjusted accordingly to whatever you think is reasonable for your situation, or the region where you live.

Another possible cost when renting a place is renter's insurance. For renter's insurance, have the students estimate the value of their possessions. These possessions may include a bike, furniture, CDs, jewelry, collections, clothes, electronics, etc. Next, have the students multiply that amount by 1% or .01 to get the yearly renter's insurance expense. Then, divide the yearly expense by 12 to get the monthly renter's insurance expense. For example, if someone has $5000 worth of possessions, then $5000 x .01 = $50. $50 divided by 12 is $4.17 per month for renter's insurance.

An easy way to calculate renter's insurance is to pay a flat rate of $75 per year, or whatever you think is reasonable. Therefore, $75 divided by 12 is $6.25 per month for renter's insurance. The concept of renter's insurance is more important than the exact amount.

A couple of other things to remember when calculating monthly rental expenses is that for this project, students calculate only regular monthly rent. This project does not include security deposit, pet deposit, or any other type of deposit. Depending on your scope and goals, you may want to mention that first month's rent will cost double because of the security deposit, instead of just the regular monthly rent. Also, some places have one or two months rent free if a year's lease is signed. If that situation occurs, just add up the ten or eleven month's rent and divide by 12 to get the average regular monthly rent expense. Or, assuming the months of free rent are over, the students can use the regular monthly rent amount to simulate what the rent would be for the majority of the time.

I found the students loved finding a place to live. It gave them some insight to how much it costs to "put a roof over your head." Also, it gave them a sense of independence because they were in the virtual process of living on their own. There was much research, debate, and math being done when deciding if they wanted to live by themselves, have a roommate, or have several roommates.

Example Problems: Calculating Monthly Rental Expenses

Example 1

Antonio has an apartment. He pays $450 a month for rent, $60 a month for heat, $30 a month for water, and $45 a month for electricity.

A. What is Antonio's total monthly rental expense?

Answer: $450 + $60 + $30 + $45 = $585.00

B. What is Antonio's total yearly rental expense?

Answer: $585 x 12 = $7020.00

Example 2

Armond's insurance company charges him 1.5% of the value of his property for rental insurance for the year. Armond owns $9800 worth of property.

A. What is Armond's yearly rental insurance?

Answer: $9800 x .015 = $147.00

B. What is Armond's monthly rental insurance?

Answer: $147 divided by 12 = $12.25

Example 3

Brooke and Kelly share an apartment. They agree to split all costs. They pay $525 a month for rent, $65 a month for heat, $37 a month for water, and $51 a month for electricity. Together they pay renters insurance of $20 per month.

A. What is the total cost each month?

Answer: $525 + $65 + $37 + $51 + $20 = $698.00

B. What does just Brooke pay each month?

Answer: $698 divided by 2 = $349.00

Student Practice Problems: Calculating Monthly Rental Expenses

1. Ming has an apartment. She pays $525 a month for rent, $45 a month for heat, $35 a month for water, and $40 a month for electricity.

   A. What is Ming's total monthly rental expense?

   B. What is Ming's total yearly rental expense?

2. DeWayne's insurance company charges him 1.5% of the value of his property for rental insurance for the year. DeWayne owns $7550 worth of property.

   A. What is DeWayne's yearly rental insurance?

   B. What is DeWayne's monthly rental insurance?

3. Antwon and Cindy share an apartment. They agree to split all costs. They pay $625 a month for rent, $55 a month for heat, $47 a month for water, and $41 a month for electricity. Together they pay renters insurance of $20 per month.

   A. What is the total cost each month?

   B. What does just Antwon pay each month?

Hands-On Student Activity: Calculate Your Monthly Rental Expenses

1. Calculate your monthly rent payment for your living situation. You may be living alone or sharing an apartment. Also, calculate your monthly utilities (heat, water, and electric) if they are not included in your rent. If your utilities are not included in your rent payment, reasonably calculate/estimate your monthly utilities.

2. Calculate your monthly renter's insurance (1.5% of value of your property).

3. Write a check for each bill.

4. Enter the amounts in your checkbook and subtract them from the previous balance.

5. Enter the amount of your bills in your monthly budget organizer (optional).

6. Tell why you chose the place that you did and describe any advantages or disadvantages. Also, what did you learn from this activity that may help you in the future?

____

____

____

____

____

____

____

____

____

____

Phone, Television, and Internet Expenses

Figure 4-2

Introduction

There are many options available for different combinations of phone, TV, and internet. Some people have a phone/TV/internet package deal. Some people have a TV/internet package with one provider and have their phone carrier with another provider. Some people have different providers for each of their phone, TV, and internet. Figure 4-2 is an example of some of the phone options available.

Depending on if the students have roommates or live by themselves, there are many outcomes for having a phone, TV, and internet. Calculating the monthly phone, TV, and internet expenses can be as holistic or as simple as you want. Therefore, depending on your scope and goals, the phone, TV, and internet costs can be researched or they can be estimated. The concept of having a phone, TV, and internet expense is more important than the exact amount.

Researching the phone, TV, and internet providers, along with the costs associated with those providers, can be exciting. Researching these luxuries can come from the internet, newspapers, catalogs, phone calls, TV, phone books, parents, word of mouth, and other ways. There are many providers that would love the student's business. When students research the providers, they may want to think about the different options each provider gives.

For example, when researching a phone plan, students may want to think about:

- Long distance charges
- Times they mostly call
- Free night/weekend calling
- How much the actual phone costs, or is it free
- Friends and family
- Possible sharing with roommates
- Cost
- Time Commitment—1, 2, or 3 years
- Other possible options

When researching a TV provider, the students may want to think about:

- Cable
- Dish
- Premium channels
- Add-on channels
- Cost
- Time Commitment—1, 2, or 3 years
- Other possible options

When researching an internet provider, students may want to think about:

- Speed and usage
- Cost
- Time Commitment—1, 2, or 3 years
- Other possible options

There are several other expenses that need mentioning. The first one relates to the actual cost of the phone. Some cell phone plans will give you a free phone with a 2 year membership and some cell phone plans will charge you for the initial phone and then give you their membership. If the phone provider charges the students for the initial phone, then the students may or may not want to add that into their budget because the cost of the initial phone was only a one-time expense. The second phone expense relates to the phone bill. If students choose a cell phone plan for a flat rate of, say $49.99 a month, there is a federal usage surcharge and a cell phone provider usage surcharge. These two surcharges are about $4.00 each. Whether you choose to incorporate them is up to you and your students. Also, there is a tax on the monthly phone bill. Whether you choose to incorporate the tax is also up to you and your students, depending on your scope and goals. Taxes will vary according to each state and region. Further, do the students want to have cell phone insurance, in case they break it or drop it in a puddle?

Lastly, there may be an installation fee or a hook-up fee associated with getting the phone, TV, and internet. This fee could be included in the monthly expense for this month or skipped because the installation fee is a one-time charge and not a regular monthly charge.

When I brought in newspapers, catalogs, and other materials for the students to use for hands-on research, the students were very excited. Although the phone, TV, and internet are luxuries, they were extremely important to the students, which was not surprising.

Example Problems: Calculating Monthly Phone, TV, and Internet Expenses

1. Tong, Juan, Patrick, and Bill share a 4 bedroom apartment. They have a phone/TV/internet package deal. The total monthly bill comes to $141.14.

    A. What does each roommate pay for the month?

    Answer: $141.14 divided by 4 = $35.29 (To the Nearest Penny)

2. Alicia and Jennifer share a 2 bedroom apartment. They each have their own cell phone. Alicia pays $73.00 per month for her cell phone and Jennifer pays $89.00 per month for her cell phone. They also share a TV/internet package that costs $74.00 per month.

    A. What is Alicia's cost per month for phone, TV, and internet?

    Answer: $74.00 divided by 2 = $37.00
    $37.00 + $73.00 = $110.00

    B. What is Jennifer's cost per month for phone, TV, and internet?

    Answer: $74.00 divided by 2 = $37.00
    $37.00 + $89.00 = $126.00

3. Mary can't decide which offer to take. Offer 1 is a package deal for phone/TV/internet for $117.53 a month for a 1 year subscription. Offer 2 is to pay $65.95 a month for phone, $55.47 a month for TV, and $25.50 a month for internet.

    A. How much will Mary pay a year for option 1?

    Answer: $117.53 x 12 = $1410.36

    B. How much will Mary pay a year for option 2?

    Answer: $65.95 + $55.47 + $25.50 = $146.92
    $146.92 x 12 = $1763.04

    C. Which offer is the better deal and by how much?

    Answer: Offer 1 is the better deal by $352.68 per year
    $1763.04—$1410.36 = $352.68

Student Practice Problems: Calculating Monthly Phone, TV, and Internet Expenses

1. Alvin, Landiran, and Reynold share a 3 bedroom apartment. They have a phone/TV/internet package deal. The total monthly bill comes to $137.84.

    A. What does each roommate pay for the month?

2. Becky and Holly share a 2 bedroom apartment. They each have their own cell phone. Becky pays $63.00 per month for her cell phone and Holly pays $69.00 for her cell phone. They also share a TV/internet package that costs $84.00 per month.

    A. What is Becky's cost per month for phone, TV, and internet?

    B. What is Holly's cost per month for phone, TV, and internet?

3. Gary can't decide which offer to take. Offer 1 is a package deal for phone/TV/internet for $110.00 a month for a 1 year subscription. Offer 2 is to pay $55.00 a month for phone, $45.00 a month for TV, and $15.00 a month for internet.

    A. How much will Gary pay a year for option 1?

    B. How much will Gary pay a year for option 2?

    C. Which offer is the better deal and by how much?

Hands-On Student Activity: Calculate Your Monthly Phone, TV, and Internet Expenses

1. Calculate your phone, TV, and internet expenses for the month.

    A. Cost of the phone (if any)________________

    B. Cost of the monthly phone plan________________

    C. Possible surcharge fees______________

    D. Possible tax___________________

    E. Internet expense___________________________

    F. TV expense______________________________

    G. Possible installation and/or hook-up fee expense/s___________

    H. Total monthly expenses for phone, TV, and internet___________________

2. Write a check to your providers for each of the expenses you need to pay and subtract those amounts in your checkbook.

3. Document those expenses in your monthly budget organizer (optional).

4. Describe why you chose the phone, TV, and internet provider/s that you did. What advantages or disadvantages did you discover? Also, what did you learn from this activity that may help you in the future?

____

____

____

____

____

____

____

____

____

____

Auto and Other Related Expenses

Figure 4-3

Introduction

Since people need reliable transportation to get to their jobs and other obligations, the students are going to also purchase a vehicle during this project. Since most people don't have the thousands of dollars in cash it costs to purchase a vehicle, they are going to have to borrow (or finance) the amount of money the vehicle costs. Figure 4-3 is an example of a one type of vehicle advertisement.

Calculating the monthly auto expense can be as holistic or as easy as your situation prescribes. For a more holistic approach, the students can research on the internet, newspapers, or magazines to find vehicles that they like and are in their price range. Like finding a place to rent or finding a phone, bring in newspapers, catalogs, and anything else the students can use to give them hands-on options to find a vehicle to finance.

There are many choices available for financing a vehicle that students will find when they are researching. For example, there could be 0% financing for 60 months, 3.99% for three years, or other incentives that are offered from dealerships selling vehicles. Each dealership has its own unique financing offer. Therefore, if students find a vehicle they like from a dealership, they can finance the vehicle through that dealership.

Another possible choice to finance is if students find vehicles being sold from a person instead of a dealership. If this occurs, then the buyer (student) will have to borrow money from a bank or a credit union. The students can use any rate you feel is reasonable, or use the rate that was researched for that particular lending institution.

When financing (borrowing money), the lender is going to charge interest unless the buyer (student) finds an opportunity where the offer is 0% for 60 or 72 months(usually, that only gets offered with a new vehicle purchase which is typically too high of a monthly payment for a student at this time). Interest is the money you owe to the borrower for having them lend you money to buy a vehicle. For example, if someone borrows $3000.00, he/she will have to pay back $3000.00 plus interest. Interest, for this activity, will be calculated using the simple interest formula of I = PxRxT. Interest is calculated by multiplying the principal (money borrowed) x the rate (as a decimal) x time (in years).

For a more simplistic approach to getting a vehicle, just estimate a reasonable monthly expense for the automobile. It's the concept of financing and having a vehicle payment that is more important than the exact amount. One option to explain financing to younger students is to tell them this: "Suppose you wanted a pizza. You searched and searched for the perfect pizza. All of a sudden, you found Peppy, the man selling the perfect pizza. You looked at that perfect pizza and wanted it. You asked Peppy how much that perfect pizza cost. Peppy said the price was $10.00. You said that you didn't have ten dollars. Peppy said that was O.K. He said he would give you the perfect pizza right now while it is still hot and ready to eat and all you have to do is give him $1.00 per month for the next twelve months. You realize that would cost a total of twelve dollars instead of ten. You said O.K. because you could easily come up with $1.00 per month for the next twelve months since you didn't have the ten dollars right now for Peppy. So, you took the perfect pizza." Financing can be described any way you feel is applicable to get the concept across to your students.

There are many opportunities for developing financing and interest concepts depending on your goals and the age of your students. With so many different financing opportunities available, it is good to have the students compare and contrast the different financing options.

There are many other expenses that come with maintaining a vehicle. These expenses may include repairs, cleaning, insurance, gas, oil, license renewal, license plate renewal, and more. For this activity, along with the monthly vehicle payment, the other auto expenses that will be used are insurance, gas, and oil. These four monthly expenses (car payment, insurance, gas, and oil) are being used because these are the expenses that are most consistent each month. Insurance is good to have and some states require insurance coverage (at least liability). However, depending on your scope and goals, include any vehicle expenses you feel are relevant. Also, depending on what state you line in, use whatever relevant interest rates and sales tax rates you feel are applicable for the practice problems and hands-on student activities.

I found the students energized and enthusiastic about financing a vehicle. They had an authentic realization of the cost of a vehicle, the cost of maintaining a vehicle, and the price associated with the different varieties of vehicles. It was fun to watch the students find a vehicle that they could afford, and at the same time, met their style requirements. The math involved in the process of financing and maintaining a vehicle solidified the real-life responsibility that is associated with the privilege of driving.

Example Problems: Calculating Monthly Auto Expenses

Example 1

Bashiek bought a Ford Ranger for $8285.00 plus 5% sales tax. He financed the vehicle through a bank loan at 7% interest for 3 years.

A. What is Bashiek's principal to be financed (amount he will borrow)?
   Answer: $8285 + tax =
   $8285 + ($8285 x .05) =
   $8285 + $414.25 = $8699.25
B. What i`s Bashiek's interest rate for financing?
   Answer: 7%
C. What is the length of time he has to pay his loan?
   Answer: 3 years (36 months)
D. What is Bashiek's interest amount?
   Answer: I = PxRxT
   $8699.25 x .07 x 3 = $1826.84 (rounded to the penny)
E. What is the total amount to be financed from the bank?
   Answer: principal + interest = $8699.25 + $1826.84 = $10,526.09
F. What is Bashiek's monthly car payment to the bank?
   Answer: $10,526.09 divided by 36 = $292.39

Example 2

LaQuisha bought a 2001 Camero for $4570. Her insurance company charges her 5% of that amount for insurance for the year.

A. What is LaQuisha's yearly insurance expense?
   Answer: $4570 x .05 = $228.50

B. What is LaQuisha's monthly insurance expense?
   Answer: $228.50 divided by 12 = $19.04 (rounded to the penny)

Example 3

Juan calculates that he uses 1.75 gallons of gas per day going to work and back. He goes to work about 22 days per month. Gas is $4.25 per gallon. He also gets a $23.00 oil change every three months.

A. What is Juan's monthly gas expense?
   Answer: 1.75 x $4.25 x 22 = $163.63 (rounded to the penny)

B. What is Juan's monthly oil expense?

   Answer: $23.00 divided 3 = $7.67 (rounded to the penny)

Student Practice Problems: Calculating Monthly Auto Expenses

1. Through a local bank, calculate the monthly payment to finance a vehicle that costs $6500.00 at 7% interest over 4 years. To do that, calculate:

    A. Sales Tax (5% of car cost)______________

    B. Car cost with tax (principal)____________________

    C. Interest over 4 years (principal x rate x time)__________________

    D. Total car cost with interest_________________

    E. How many months are in 4 years?______________

    F. Car cost per month (D divided by E)_________________

2. Calculate the car insurance from problem 1. Car insurance per year is 5% of the cost of the car before tax and interest.

    A. What is the cost of car insurance for one year?

    B. What is the cost of car insurance for one month?

3. Calculate the gas and oil expense per month using the criteria that you will use 1.5 gallons of gas per day at $4.30 per gallon for 20 days per month. One oil change every three months is needed. Oil changes are $23.95 each.

    A. What is the monthly gas expense?

    B. What is the monthly oil expense?

Hands-On Student Activity: Calculate Your Monthly Auto Expenses

1. Calculate the monthly payment for the vehicle you choose. If you finance your vehicle through a dealership, calculate your monthly payment with your dealership information.

If you don't finance your loan through a dealership, you have to finance your loan through your local bank or credit union. The bank/credit union charges you a 6% interest rate over 4 years.

A. What is the year, make, and model of your vehicle?____________________

B. Car Cost (without tax)__________________

C. Sales Tax (5% of car cost)______________

D. Car cost with tax (principal)_____________________

E. Interest over 4 years (principal x rate x time)__________________

F. Total car cost with interest__________________

G. How many months are in 4 years?______________

H. Car cost per month?__________________

2. Calculate your car insurance. Car insurance per year is 5% of the cost of the vehicle before tax and interest.

A. What is the cost of your car insurance for one year?

B. What is the cost of your car insurance for one month?

3. Calculate your gas expense per month using the criteria that you will use 2 gallons of gas per day at \$4.23 per gallon for 21 days per month.

4. Calculate your oil expense per month using the criteria that you will need 1 oil change every 3 months. Each oil change is $25.00

5. Write a check out for each expense above and enter them into your checkbook.

6. Document your expenses in your monthly budget organizer (optional).

7. Why did you choose the vehicle that you did? What are the advantages and disadvantages of your vehicle? Also, what did you learn from this activity that may help you in the future?

____

____

____

____

____

____

____

____

____

____

____

____

____

____

____

____

____

____

Clothing Expenses

Figure 4-4

Introduction

Another expense that people encounter is a clothing expense. Some jobs require a uniform that the employees have to supply and some jobs help pay for some of the uniform requirements. Some jobs want their employees to dress in a "business" fashion and some in a "business casual" fashion. Further, some jobs require you to wear durable clothes, steel toed boots, and have some warm weather gear. No matter what the job, there will be some clothing expenses related to that job. Figure 4-4 is an example of a clothing store advertisement.

Everyone shops for clothes differently. Some people frequently buy a couple of things at a time. Some people buy many things at one time only a couple of times per year. Whatever a person's process is for maintaining their attire, there is an average monthly cost to buying clothes.

When shopping for clothes, it seems that no matter what store you go to there is always some type of sale. Either the store is having a "percent off" sale, a "buy one get one free" sale, a "buy one get the next for half price" sale, or having a "fraction" sale (1/2 off or 1/3 off).

Calculating the monthly clothing expenses can be as holistic or as easy as your situation prescribes. Calculating clothing expenses can be as real-life as you want it to be or as easy as you want it to be, depending on your goals and age of your students. For a real-life experience, similar to finding a place to rent or finding a vehicle, have the students research clothing items on-line, or by bringing in some newspapers, catalogs, and other literature with clothing prices that students can look at.

Calculating clothing expenses can also be made easy. For younger students, estimating a monthly expense may be a viable option. The amount of the monthly clothing expense is not as important as knowing there is a monthly average expense for clothing.

I found that the students were energized when they had to find an outfit for their job. They felt empowered that they could wear what they wanted. Also, the students thought hard about what attire would be appropriate for their occupation and not just want to look cool for their friends. The students also realized how much clothes actually cost. There is a lot of fashion and math involved in this part of the project.

Example Problems: Calculating Clothing Expenses

Example 1

Margarita went to Shopko to buy a sweater and a scarf. The sweater cost $19.95 and the scarf cost $9.95.

A. What is the total cost of the items before tax?

Answer: $19.95 + $9.95 = $29.90

B. What is the sales tax for the items (5% of the total)?

Answer: $29.90 x .05 = $1.50 (rounded to the penny)

C. What is the total cost of the items including tax?

Answer: $29.90 + $1.50 = $31.40

D. If Margarita paid with two $20 bills, what does she get for change?

Answer: $40.00—$31.40 = $8.60

Example 2

Meng went to the Tommy Store to buy a coat. The coat regularly cost $49.90. It was on sale for 1/3 off when Meng got to the store.

A. How much is 1/3 off?

Answer: $49.90 x 1/3 = $16.63 (rounded to the penny)

B. What is the sale price of the coat?

Answer: $49.90—$16.63 = $33.27

C. What would the sales tax be on the coat (5% tax)?

Answer: $33.27 x .05 = $1.66 (rounded to the penny)

D. What is the final cost of the coat?

Answer: $33.27 + $1.66 = $34.93

Example 3

Ken and Beneita went to Dayton's. Dayton's was having a 20% off sale. They bought $87.50 worth of clothing before the discount.

A. How much is the discount?

Answer: $87.50 x .20 = $17.50

B. What is the price after discount?

Answer: $87.50—$17.50 = $70.00

C. What is the sales tax (5% tax)?

Answer: $70.00 x .05 = $3.50

D. What is the total cost including sales tax?

Answer: $70.00 + $3.50 = $73.50

Student Practice Problems: Calculating Clothing Expenses

1. Yolanda went to Sears to buy a pair of jeans and a top. The jeans cost $29.95 and the top cost $10.95.

    A. What is the total cost of the items before tax?

    B. What is the sales tax for the items (5% of the total)?

    C. What is the total cost of the items including tax?

    D. If Yolanda paid with a $20 bill and three $10 bills, what does she get for change?

2. Bernard went to Target to buy a suit. The suit regularly cost $129.99. It was on sale for 1/3 off when Bernard got to the store.

    A. How much is 1/3 off?

    B. What is the sale price of the coat?

    C. What would the sales tax be on the coat (5% tax)?

    D. What is the final cost of the coat?

3. Tammy went to JC Penny. JC Penny was having a 20% off sale. She bought $67.45 worth of clothing before the discount.

    A. What is the discount?

    B. What is the price after discount?

    C. What is the sales tax (5% tax)?

    D. What is the total cost including sales tax?

Hands-On Student Activity: Calculate Your Monthly Clothing Expenses

1. Buy one outfit for yourself that your occupation would want you to wear. Include things such as pants, shirts, shoes, socks, undergarments, and possible jewelry/belts. Don't forget about the sales and discounts.

ITEM	COST
______________________________	______________
______________________________	______________
______________________________	______________
______________________________	______________
______________________________	______________
______________________________	______________
______________________________	______________
______________________________	______________
______________________________	______________
______________________________	______________

TOTAL COST________________________________

SALES TAX (5%)____________________________

TOTAL COST WITH TAX_____________________

2. Write a check, to the store of your choice, for this months clothing expense.
3. Document the expense in the monthly budget organizer (optional).
4. Why did you choose the clothing that you did? Also, what did you learn from this activity that may help you in the future?

____

____

____

____

____

____

____

____

Payment Plan Expenses

Figure 4-5

Introduction

When most people move into a new house or apartment, they usually need some type of appliance, furniture, or electronic item. The stores that sell these items usually have some type of financing or payment plan. These stores offer these payment plans because they know that most people don't have that kind of cash to pay for the whole item at once. Therefore, the students are going to finance, or have a payment plan, for some type of appliance (stove, refrigerator, washer, dryer, etc.), piece of furniture (bed, dresser, couch, chair, etc), or electronic item (stereo, TV, etc.). Each store will have different incentives, and payment plans available. Some stores may offer a plan that says "pay no interest for two years." Figure 4-5 is an advertisement from an appliance store.

Calculating the monthly payment plan expenses can be as holistic or as easy as your situation prescribes. Calculating the payment plan for an appliance, a piece of furniture, or an electronic item can be as real-life as you want it to be or as easy as you want it to be, depending on your goals and age of your students. For a real-life experience, similar to finding a place to rent, finding a vehicle, or shopping for clothes, have the students research items on-line, or by bringing in some newspapers, catalogs, and other literature with items and prices that students can look at. The students can compare and contrast all the different prices available to them.

Calculating a payment plan can also be made relatively easy. For younger students, estimating a monthly expense may be a viable option. The amount of the monthly payment expense is not as important as knowing there is a monthly average expense for needed items.

I found that this portion of the financial literacy project incorporated some of the exciting math and processes similar to finding a vehicle. The difference was that students made their buying decisions a bit different. Instead of going for image, I found the students rationalizing what they needed the most in their apartment that would fulfill their needs. Some students said a sofa, while others said a washer and dryer. Some students knew right away and some had to think about it. Some students asked if they could split the cost of a washer. I said sure but one person has to write out the check to the business and the other person has to write out the check to the roommate.

Further, depending on your scope and goals, this is a great time to talk about establishing a credit score by financing, the importance of having a good credit score, and what a good and/or bad credit score can do for/to the students in the future.

Example Problems: Calculating Payment Plan Expenses

1. Ken bought a TV for $299.99 plus sales tax. Since he did not have the cash, he did a payment plan for 1 year at $30.00 a month.

A. How much does the TV cost if Ken paid cash (include sales tax 5%)?

Answer: $299.99 + tax
$299.99 + ($299.99 x .05)
$299.99 + $15.00 (rounded to the penny) = $314.99

B. How much did Ken pay?

Answer: $30 x 12 = $360.00

C. How much extra did it cost for Ken to have a payment plan instead of paying cash?

Answer: $360.00—$314.99 = $45.01

2. Claire works for General Electric. She could buy a microwave with all the extras for $159.50 because she is an employee there. She had to do a payment plan for $13 a month, for 18 months.

A. What would the price be after a 5% sales tax if she paid cash?

Answer: $159.50 + tax
$159.50 + ($159 x .05)
$159.50 + $7.98 (rounded to the penny) = $167.48

B. How much did it cost Claire to buy the microwave using the 18 month payment plan?

Answer: $13.00 x 18 = $234.00

C. How much extra did it cost Claire to do the payment plan for the microwave, instead of paying cash?

Answer: $234.00—$167.48 = $66.52

3. Karle wants to buy a VCR for her boyfriend Ken. Best Buy is selling one Ken wants for $249.99 with a year of free financing.

A. How much will the VCR cost with a 5% sales tax?

Answer: $249.99 + tax
$249.99 + ($249.99 x .05)
$249.99 + $12.50 (rounded to the penny) = $262.49

B. If Karle makes 12 equal payments, what will she pay each month?

Answer: $262.49 divided by 12 = $21.87 (rounded to the penny)

Student Practice Problems: Calculating Payment Plan Expenses

1. Michael bought an RCA digital camera for $599.99 plus a 5% sales tax. He did a payment plan that was for 2 years at $31.00 a month.

    A. What is the cost of the camera if Michael pays cash?

    B. How much did Michael pay?

    C. How much more did the camera cost using the payment plan?

2. Bobby Jo works for an electronics store. She could buy a TV for $899.99 plus a 5% sales tax. She had to use the electronics store's payment plan for $45 a month, for 24 months.

    A. What would the price for the TV be after a 5% sales tax if she paid cash?

    B. How much did it cost Bobby Jo using the 24 month payment plan?

    C. How much extra did it cost Bobby Jo on the payment plan?

3. Kendra wants to buy a VCR for her father. Best Buy is selling one Kendra wants for $349.99 with a year of free financing.

    A. How much will the VCR cost with a 5% sales tax?

    B. If Kendra makes 12 equal payments, what will she pay each month?

Hands-On Student Activity: Calculate Your Monthly Payment Plan Expenses

Select any item you need for your apartment. These items may include a refrigerator, stove, washer, dryer, stereo, furniture, TV, bedroom furniture, etc. You may purchase these items by yourself or share the expense with a roommate. If you share the expense, decide which person should write the check to the business and which person should write the check to the other roommate for half the expense.

1. What is the item you chose to purchase?

2. What is the price of your item, including a 5% sales tax?

3. The store where you purchased the item gives you free financing for two years. Calculate the monthly payments to pay off this item over the next two years.

4. Write a check for the item and subtract that amount in your checkbook.

5. Document that amount in you monthly budget organizer (optional).

6. Why did you choose the item/s that you did? Also, what did you learn from this activity that may help you in the future

____

____

____

____

____

____

____

____

____

____

____

____

Food Expenses

Figure 4-6

Introduction

An obvious monthly expense is food. Having the students plan their own meals will probably be a new experience. Most students currently have their meals planned for them. All they have to do is show up at the right location at the prescribed time, and the meal is ready for them.

Grocery shopping is something everyone has to do eventually. Some people grocery shop once per week. Some people shop every couple of days. Further, some people shop every day, depending on what they feel like eating that day. Figure 4-6 is an example of a grocery store's pasta advertising.

Calculating food expenses can be as holistic or as simple as you want, depending on your scope and goals, and age of your students. For a more holistic approach to calculating food expenses, do some research on different types of foods on-line or in stores. Also, you could bring in flyers, newspapers, or other literature with food prices and food specials that students can look at. You may want to do some cost analysis for different foods.

For younger students, estimating a monthly food expense may be a viable option. The concept of knowing there will be a monthly food expense is more important than the exact amount calculated.

This activity has students calculate the daily food costs for breakfast, lunch, and supper for seven days. The seven days are totaled, and then that total is multiplied by four to get the average monthly food expense.

When doing this activity, have the students hit as many food groups as they can each meal every day. Be flexible, to an extent. Students will mention about splitting pizzas, or having leftovers, or going out to eat, or having a gallon of milk last all week. All these things are worth discussing because they are real-life examples of how we eat. For example, one question I encountered was "Since pizza has most of the food groups in it, can I eat half a pizza for lunch and the other half for supper?" I couldn't say no, because that is exactly what I have done in the past. Further, if students buy a five pound bag of apples, they could have 1 or 2 apples per day for a week to meet the objective of trying to include the fruit group everyday. Therefore, you may want some flexibility in this exercise. Again, the concept of knowing there will be a monthly food expense is more important than the exact amount calculated. Figure 4-7 is a great example of one of the ways to keep food expenses low when there are "specials" being offered. A couple of dollars of pasta and pasta sauce can go a long way.

Figure 4-7

Further, even though you may have to be flexible with the types of breakfasts, lunches, and suppers that the students are planning, you may want to stress the benefits of eating healthy or at least semi-healthy. For example, some students asked me if they could buy a dozen "day old" donuts and eat those for breakfast everyday. I said no because even though they found a cheap breakfast that fit into their budget, eating donuts everyday for breakfast is not reasonable, not to mention very unhealthy. So, again, stress the fact of finding a "happy medium" between economical and healthy. Lastly, this may be a good time to integrate a health class with the health and/or the wellness teacher.

I found the students getting real creative in this activity. Food costs a lot of money. So, some students got real frugal. I had students ask many interesting questions. Depending on your goals, time, and age of your students, discuss what you and your students think is reasonable for eating and how that eating will progress through the week.

Example Problems: Calculating Food Expenses

Example 1

Mint chocolate bars come in a 24 ounce bag for $3.89.

A. What is the unit price per ounce?

Answer: $3.89 divided by 24 = $.16 per ounce (rounded to the penny)

Example 2

America's Choice grape juice is two 16 ounce cans for $3.00. Flavorade grape juice is three 12 ounce cans for $3.50.

A. What are the unit prices per ounce for each brand?

Answer: America's Choice
$3.00 divided by 32 = $.09 per ounce (rounded to the penny)

Answer: Flavorade
$3.50 divided by 36 = $.10 per ounce (rounded to the penny)

B. What is the better buy?

Answer: America's Choice

Example 3

For a recipe, Kellie needs 2 pounds of hamburger for every 7 people. The hamburger is $2.49 per pound. She is having 21 people over for dinner.

A. How many pounds of hamburger should she buy?

Answer: 21 divided by 7 = 3
3 x 2 = 6 pounds

B. How much will she spend on hamburger?

Answer: 6 x $2.49 = $14.94

Student Practice Problems: Calculating Food Expenses

Example 1

Chicken thighs/legs come in a package of 3 for $3.99.

A. What is the unit price per thigh/leg portion?

Example 2

Dean's yogurt is 10, 8 ounce containers for $5.50. Doug's yogurt is 8, 12 ounce containers for $6.00.

A. What are the unit prices per ounce for each brand?

Dean's Doug's

B. What is the better buy?

Example 3

For a recipe, Troyell needs 3 pounds of chicken for every 9 people. The chicken is $1.49 per pound. He is having 36 people over for dinner.

A. How many pounds of chicken should he buy?

B. How much will he spend on chicken?

Hands-On Student Activity: Calculate Your Monthly Food Expenses

Here are two more simple examples to get you started.

Example 1: Suppose you go shopping. In the shopping cart you put:

Item	Cost	Unit Cost
1 gallon of milk	$3.00	$.19/cup
1 box of cereal	$3.00	$.50/serving
1 bunch of bananas	$2.00	$.40/banana

So, the total bill for the items above is $8.00. However, that $8.00 is going to be distributed among several meals. For example, if you have a bowl of cereal, with a cup of milk, and a banana for breakfast, that breakfast only cost $.19 + $.50 + $.40 = $1.09. As you can see, a box of cereal, milk, and a bunch of bananas can be spread out throughout several breakfasts for only $1.09 per breakfast. Plus, you used the fruit group, the grain group, and the dairy group in that morning's meal.

Example 2: Suppose you go shopping. In the shopping cart you put:

Item	Cost	Unit Cost
3 pizzas	$9.99	$3.33/pizza

The bill for the items is $9.99. However, that $9.99 is going to be spread among several meals. You can have a half of a pizza for lunch and have the other half of the pizza for supper the next night. $3.33 divided by 2 = $1.67 per meal and you have two pizzas left for some other time.

To calculate your monthly food expense, plan and calculate your food expenses for breakfast, lunch, and supper for each day, Monday through Sunday. Use the "unit cost" strategy like in example 1 and 2. When planning your meals, try to stay as close to the recommended daily allowance as possible each day. All snacks must be written in as well.

Below is an example of the food groups and the recommended daily portions for each food group.

Bread, Cereal, Rice, and Pasta = BG (bread group)

Grain products like bread, cereal, rice, and pasta are good for you. They are important sources of vitamins and minerals. Breads, cereals, rice, and pasta are also good sources of carbohydrates like starch and fiber. (6 Servings Per Day)

Vegetables = VG (vegetable group)

Vegetables are a source of important vitamins, minerals and carbohydrates. Vegetables differ in the vitamins and minerals they contain. It is important to eat a variety of vegetables. (3 Servings Per Day). Figure 4-8 shows a variety of delicious vegetables.

Fruits = FG (fruit group)

Fruits are important sources of vitamins and carbohydrates like fiber and sugar. They are low in calories and naturally sweet. Fruits and their juices are good sources of water, too. Different fruits contain different vitamins, so it is important to eat a variety of fruits. (2 Servings Per Day)

Meat, Poultry, Fish, Dry Beans, Eggs, and Nuts = PG (protein group)

Meat, poultry, fish, dry beans, eggs, and nuts are important sources of protein, iron, zinc, and B vitamins. This group includes plant foods and animal foods. (2 Servings Per Day)

Milk, Yogurt, and Cheese = MG (milk group)

Milk and foods made from milk are the best sources of the mineral calcium. They also provide us with vitamin A, protein, and phosphorus. The foods in this group are important because all of the nutrients work together to keep our bones strong and healthy. It may be difficult to get enough calcium unless we include these foods in our diets. We can make sure we get the milk and calcium we need by making puddings and soups with milk. (3 Servings Per Day)

Fats, Oils, Sweets, Extras = Extras

Fats, oils, and sweets give us calories. Fats and oils like salad dressings, mayonnaise, butter, margarine and lard tend to be high in calories because of the fat they contain. Sweets like candy, soft drinks, syrups, jams, and jellies are made mostly of sugars. Extras also include chips, catsup, mustard, miracle whip, cake, frosting, syrup, etc. This group should be used sparingly.

It is also recommended that you drink 8 cups of water per day.

Figure 4-8

Monday Meals

	Breakfast		Lunch		Supper	
	Item	Cost	Item	Cost	Item	Cost
BG						
VG						
FG						
PG						
MG						
Extra						
Cost						

Total Cost for Monday___________

Tuesday Meals

	Breakfast		Lunch		Supper	
	Item	Cost	Item	Cost	Item	Cost
BG	______	______	______	______	______	______
	______	______	______	______	______	______
	______	______	______	______	______	______
	______	______	______	______	______	______
VG	______	______	______	______	______	______
	______	______	______	______	______	______
	______	______	______	______	______	______
	______	______	______	______	______	______
FG	______	______	______	______	______	______
	______	______	______	______	______	______
	______	______	______	______	______	______
	______	______	______	______	______	______
PG	______	______	______	______	______	______
	______	______	______	______	______	______
	______	______	______	______	______	______
	______	______	______	______	______	______
MG	______	______	______	______	______	______
	______	______	______	______	______	______
	______	______	______	______	______	______
	______	______	______	______	______	______
Extra	______	______	______	______	______	______
	______	______	______	______	______	______
	______	______	______	______	______	______
	______	______	______	______	______	______
Cost	________		________		________	

Total Cost for Tuesday__________

Wednesday Meals

	Breakfast		Lunch		Supper	
	Item	Cost	Item	Cost	Item	Cost
BG	________	________	________	________	________	________
	________	________	________	________	________	________
	________	________	________	________	________	________
	________	________	________	________	________	________
VG	________	________	________	________	________	________
	________	________	________	________	________	________
	________	________	________	________	________	________
	________	________	________	________	________	________
FG	________	________	________	________	________	________
	________	________	________	________	________	________
	________	________	________	________	________	________
	________	________	________	________	________	________
PG	________	________	________	________	________	________
	________	________	________	________	________	________
	________	________	________	________	________	________
	________	________	________	________	________	________
MG	________	________	________	________	________	________
	________	________	________	________	________	________
	________	________	________	________	________	________
	________	________	________	________	________	________
Extra	________	________	________	________	________	________
	________	________	________	________	________	________
	________	________	________	________	________	________
	________	________	________	________	________	________
Cost	__________		__________		__________	

Total Cost for Wednesday______________

Thursday Meals

	Breakfast Item	Breakfast Cost	Lunch Item	Lunch Cost	Supper Item	Supper Cost
BG						
VG						
FG						
PG						
MG						
Extra						
Cost						

Total Cost for Thursday___________

Friday Meals

	Breakfast		Lunch		Supper	
	Item	Cost	Item	Cost	Item	Cost
BG	________	________	________	________	________	________
	________	________	________	________	________	________
	________	________	________	________	________	________
	________	________	________	________	________	________
VG	________	________	________	________	________	________
	________	________	________	________	________	________
	________	________	________	________	________	________
	________	________	________	________	________	________
FG	________	________	________	________	________	________
	________	________	________	________	________	________
	________	________	________	________	________	________
	________	________	________	________	________	________
PG	________	________	________	________	________	________
	________	________	________	________	________	________
	________	________	________	________	________	________
	________	________	________	________	________	________
MG	________	________	________	________	________	________
	________	________	________	________	________	________
	________	________	________	________	________	________
	________	________	________	________	________	________
Extra	________	________	________	________	________	________
	________	________	________	________	________	________
	________	________	________	________	________	________
	________	________	________	________	________	________
Cost	__________		__________		__________	

Total Cost for Friday__________

Saturday Meals

	Breakfast		Lunch		Supper	
	Item	Cost	Item	Cost	Item	Cost
BG						
VG						
FG						
PG						
MG						
Extra						
Cost						

Total Cost for Saturday__________

Sunday Meals

	Breakfast		Lunch		Supper	
	Item	Cost	Item	Cost	Item	Cost
BG	______	______	______	______	______	______
	______	______	______	______	______	______
	______	______	______	______	______	______
	______	______	______	______	______	______
VG	______	______	______	______	______	______
	______	______	______	______	______	______
	______	______	______	______	______	______
	______	______	______	______	______	______
FG	______	______	______	______	______	______
	______	______	______	______	______	______
	______	______	______	______	______	______
	______	______	______	______	______	______
PG	______	______	______	______	______	______
	______	______	______	______	______	______
	______	______	______	______	______	______
	______	______	______	______	______	______
MG	______	______	______	______	______	______
	______	______	______	______	______	______
	______	______	______	______	______	______
	______	______	______	______	______	______
Extra	______	______	______	______	______	______
	______	______	______	______	______	______
	______	______	______	______	______	______
	______	______	______	______	______	______
Cost	________		________		________	

Total Cost for Sunday__________

Daily Totals For The Week of Meals

Monday Total____________

Tuesday Total ____________

Wednesday Total __________

Thursday Total ____________

Friday Total ______________

Saturday Total ____________

Sunday Total _____________

Weekly Total

Monday + Tuesday + Wednesday + Thursday + Friday + Saturday + Sunday ___________

Monthly Total

Weekly Total x 4_____________

1. Write a check to a grocery store of your choice for your average monthly food expense and subtract that amount in your checkbook.

2. Document that amount in you monthly budget organizer (optional).

3. Why did you choose the food items that you did? Also, what did you learn from this activity that may help you in the future?

____

____

____

____

____

____

____

____

Student Reflection—Essay or Oral Discussion

Try to remember all the activities that you accomplished in the consumer math section when talking about the following questions:

1. Did you have enough money for all your monthly expenses? Yes or no and why?
2. Reflect on what you learned from doing this activity? What were the most and least important things that you learned?
3. Would you recommend this activity to a friend? Why or why not?
4. What would you add or take away from this activity to make it more effective for you and why?
5. On a scale of 1-10, with 1 being not good and 10 being great, what number would you rate this activity and why?
6. Finally, on a scale of 1-10, with 1 being not good and 10 being great, how would you rate yourself in your commitment to "keeping it real" when doing this activity and why?
7. Do you think this activity will benefit you in the future? Why or why not?

CONCLUSION

Again, I have tried to make the financial literacy section in this book as real life and hands-on as possible for the students. Secondly, another of my goals was to have the students realize the type of job they needed to set goals for, when determining the type of lifestyle they would like to enjoy. Third, I think the financial literacy section is a holistic conclusion to being employed or starting your own business, like the ideas and concepts of the school store. The sooner students realize the cost of living and the finances it takes just to have food, clothes, shelter, and a few amenities, the sooner they will take their dedication to school, goal setting, and acquiring a job more seriously. Hopefully, this practical experience opened the student's eyes to that process.

This financial literacy section can be modified in many ways. There are numerous ways to integrate the financial literacy section into different content areas. It all depends on your scope and goals. The financial literacy can be made longer, shorter, harder, or easier. There are many more expenses and ideas that can be incorporated. For example, another expense that students may face, depending on their occupation, is a student loan expense. Some people graduate from higher education with some type of tuition debt. Some of the jobs the students chose probably had to have some type of higher education. Another expense could be a "surprise" vehicle expense. For example, everyone could get an expense for their vehicle like muffler, brakes, windshield, starter, alternator, tires, belt, etc.

Further discussion and reflection can be made after each activity. If the students overspend their monthly allotment, you may want them to go back and select a more reasonable choice for their apartment, phone/TV, car, clothing, appliance, and/or food items.

When I taught this financial literacy project in elementary and middle school, I used it as a tool to teach and complement the fractions, decimal, and percents concepts (Numbers and Operations). Fractions, decimals, and percents can be boring and confusing. However, if students are shown examples of how fractions, decimals, and percents are used in daily life, numbers and operations acquire more meaning and importance.

Depending on your scope and goals, this project can be graded and/or used as an assessment tool. Point values, can be given to the "Student Practice Problems" and rubrics can be made for the essays in each expense topic and the Student Reflection Essay.

ANSWER KEY TO STUDENT PRACTICE PROBLEMS

Student Practice Problems Answers: Calculating Earnings

1A. $248.00 1B. $12,896.00 5A. $687.50 5B. $35,750.00

2A. $420.00 2B. $21,840.00 6A. $890.00 6B. $46,280.00

3A. $336.50 3B. $17,498.00 7A. $1600.00 7B. $19,200.00

4A. $754.00 4B. $39,208.00 8A. $33,360.00

Student Practice Problems Answers: Calculating Monthly Net Income (Using 25% of gross income)

1A. $10,500.00 1B. $31,500.00 1C. $2625.00

2A. $7250.00 2B. $21,750.00 2C. $1812.50

3A. $4590.00 3B. $13,770.00 3C. $1147.50

Student Practice Problems Answers: Calculating Monthly Rental Expenses

1A. $645.00 1B. $7740.00

2A. $113.25 2B. $9.44 (rounded to the penny)

3A. $788.00 3B. $394.00

Student Practice Problems Answers: Calculating Monthly Phone, TV, and Internet Expenses

1A. $45.95 (rounded to the penny)

2A. $105.00 2B. $111.00

3A. $1320.00 3B. $1380.00 3C. Offer 1 is the better deal by $60.00

Student Practice Problems Answers: Calculating Monthly Auto Expenses

1A. $325.00 1B. $6825.00 1C. $1911.00 1D. $8736.00 1E. 48 1F. $182.00

2A. $325.00 2B. $27.08 (rounded to the penny)

3.A $129.00 3B. $7.98 (rounded to the penny)

Student Practice Problems Answers: Calculating Clothing Expenses

1A. \$40.90 1B. \$2.05 (rounded) 1C. \$42.95 1D. \$7.05

2A. \$43.33 2B. \$86.66 2C. \$4.33 (rounded) 2D. \$90.99

3A. \$13.49 3B. \$53.96 3C. \$2.70 (rounded) 3D. \$56.66

Student Practice Problems Answers: Calculating Payment Plan Expense

1A. \$629.99 1B. \$744.00 1C. \$114.01

2A. \$944.99 2B \$1080.00 2C. \$135.01

3A. \$367.49 (rounded to the penny) 3B. \$30.62 (rounded to the penny)

Student Practice Problems Answers: Calculating Food Expenses

1A. \$1.33 2A. Dean's = \$.07/ounce (rounded to the penny) Doug's = \$.06/ounce (rounded to the penny)

2B. Doug's

3A. 12 3B. \$17.88

SECTION 5

APPENDICIES

APPENDIX A
SCHOOL STORE BUSINESS PLANS

Simple Business Plan (Elementary)

Simple Business Plan (Junior High)

Detailed Business Plan For A School Store
- Complete A Market Analysis
- Describe Your Potential Customers, Based on Your Market Analysis
- Decide on a Business Name and Type of Business
- Start Bookkeeping
  - Sales Record
  - Ledger
  - Sample Sales, Profits, and Inventory Spreadsheet

Determine Staffing and Job Titles
Select A Location For Your Business
Plan For Equipment and Supplies
- Sample School Store Survey

Competition
Pricing
Advertising
- School Store Information Announcement
- School Store Service Announcement

Funds Needed to Start Business

SIMPLE BUSINESS PLAN (ELEMENTARY)

Business name and description:

___

___

Who are your customers?

___

___

___

What supplies will you need?

___

___

How much money do you need to start your business?

___

___

What types of employees will you need?

___

___

Where will you advertise?

___

___

How much will you charge for your product or service?

___

___

How will you keep track of money and sales?

___

___

What will you do with the profits?

___

___

SIMPLE BUSINESS PLAN (JUNIOR HIGH)

What is the name of your business? ______________________________

Type of business (manufacturer, retailer, or service provider) ______________________

What kind of records are you keeping? ______________________________

____

Where will your business be located? Who will work there? What will they be doing?

____

____

What kind of supplies/equipment do you need, and where will you get them?

____

____

____

Who are your potential customers?

____

How do you know they will buy your product or service? ______________________

____

Where else can people buy products or services like yours? What makes yours better?

____

____

Where and how will you advertise your product? Who will create the advertising?

____

____

How much money do you need to start your business (include materials and any other costs involved)?____

____

____

How much will you charge for your product or service? Will it be enough to cover your costs? Does it include a profit? ______________________________

____

DETAILED BUSINESS PLAN FOR A SCHOOL STORE

This detailed business plan includes suggested sequence, ideas, examples, and reproducible pages for integrating a school store into parts of your curriculum. The detailed business plan procedure, depth, integration, and components addressed will vary for each school depending on your needs, scope, and goals.

Complete a Market Analysis

The primary objective of a market analysis is to see if the idea of a school store is feasible. Are there features and benefits of a school store that meet some of the needs or wants of your school? If the answer is yes, then let the **Fun "In Store" For Students** begin. Here are some sample questions to ask:

- Are there features and benefits of a school store that meet your needs?
- Would people buy the products/services?
- Do the products/services have value?
- Where else can people buy products/services like ours? Can people get them near here?
- Are the product/services better or worse than those offered by businesses near here?

Information and notes about your market analysis:

____

____

____

____

____

____

____

____

____

____

____

____

____

Describe Your Potential Customers, Based on Your Market Analysis

- Average age?
- Gender (male, female, or both)?
- Student or staff member?
- What needs does the product or service meet?
- Is the price of the products/services especially important to the potential customers?

The committee or the students may have already considered the potential customer.

Information and notes about your potential customers:

Decide on a Business Name and Type of Business (may already be in progress)

Information and notes about your business name and type of business:

Start Bookkeeping

- Record all expenses and income as they occur
- Save all receipts
- Start recording/documenting/taking inventory of all things you feel necessary
- Start a checking account (optional)

Keeping accurate records from the beginning is important and best accomplished through consistency. At first, the school store coordinator may have to start bookkeeping. There will be instances where the bookkeeping will be relatively short and simple and instances where the bookkeeping will be long and involved. In time, bookkeeping may involve many things, especially sales and inventory.

Sales may need to be totaled by someone daily, weekly, or bi-monthly depending on how often the store is open, number and ability of employees, and time. Keeping accurate records and tracking where every penny goes from every store item can be tedious and time consuming. Store items may get lost, broken, or used to conduct daily business. Therefore, depending on your school's goals and objectives, you may think that learning the bookkeeping process is more important than a few missing pennies. After a system is in place, bookkeeping will be less demanding and time consuming.

Inventories give the staff an overview of items that may be overlooked, forgotten, need to be sold because of shelf life, or need to be reordered. Since taking inventory can have an effect on store profits, an inventory of school store supplies should be taken properly. Planning, employee training, and the use of standardized counting procedures may do this. The number of inventories per month may vary depending on the school's size, promotions, and the number of items for sale. Depending on the degree of sophistication in the record keeping, inventory can be totaled by the manager and/or bookkeeper to arrive at the total inventory figure. The count may need to be verified for accuracy. An advisor or another student can double-check a student's count if need be. The inventory process helps students learn counting, record keeping, and organizing skills. Your store employee's age or ability to independently accomplish this task may need to be taken into consideration. Further, using the inventory data from the items sold, there is an excellent opportunity to integrate activities into the curriculum. See appendix G for some related classroom activities.

Another great opportunity arises for the students when it comes time to possibly opening a school store checking account. You may want to choose a local bank. Find out from your school district's business office what the district's tax-exempt number is. This may help enable you to receive benefits such as inexpensive checks, free checking, start-up checks, no fees, etc. You may want to integrate into math class how to balance a checkbook, which is discussed in the Financial Literacy section of this book.

The next few pages have examples of a sales record, a ledger, and a spreadsheet. Advisors may modify these pages to meet individual needs. The "Sample Sales, Profits, and Inventory Spreadsheet" is an example of how to incorporate different categories into one spreadsheet. This is the spreadsheet I integrated into parts of the curriculum at a junior high school when I developed and operated a school store there. This spreadsheet reflects four months of sales.

Sales Record

DATE	TOTAL SALES	CLERKS

TOTAL SALES________________________

Ledger

Expenses Income

Date	**Paid to**	**Reason for Payment**	**When paid**	**Amount**	**Source**	**Balance**

Sample Sales, Profits, and Inventory Spreadsheet

Date Sold	Sept.	Oct.	Nov.	Dec.	Total	Selling	Total	Cost	Total	Total	Sub	% OF	Current	Inv	Order	# To
ITEM	# Sold	# Sold	#Sold	#Sold	Sold	Price	Sales	Price	Cost	Profit	Total	Sales	Inv	After	At	Order
ERASERS																
Regular	4	5	3	3	15	$0.50	$7.50	$0.35	$5.25	$2.25						
Wedge	2	3	5	6	16	$0.25	$4.00	$0.15	$2.40	$1.60	$3.85	1.5%				
FOAM GRIPS	18	11	10	10	49	$0.25	$12.25	$0.16	$7.84	$4.41	$4.41	1.8%				
LEAD	10	12	12	12	46	$1.00	$46.00	$0.47	$21.62	$24.38	$24.38	9.7%				
MARKERS																
Highlighters	5	6	6	5	22	$0.85	$18.70	$0.50	$11.00	$7.70						
Smelly Markers	4	5	6	7	22	$0.85	$18.70	$0.32	$7.04	$11.66	$19.36	7.7%				
PAPER																
Loose Leaf	5	5	5	5	20	$1.00	$20.00	$0.72	$14.40	$5.60						
Small Notebooks	3	3	3	3	12	$0.50	$6.00	$0.13	$1.56	$4.44						
Spiral	8	9	8	9	34	$0.75	$25.50	$0.18	$6.12	$19.38	$29.42	11.7%				
PENCILS																
Back Clicker	10	10	10	10	40	$0.65	$26.00	$0.24	$9.60	$16.40						
Colored/Big	3	4	4	3	14	$1.75	$24.50	$1.27	$17.78	$6.72						
Colored/Small	2	3	2	3	10	$1.25	$12.50	$0.79	$7.90	$4.60						
Front Clicker	11	14	9	10	43	$0.65	$27.95	$0.51	$21.93	$6.02						
Non-Sharpening Clr	2	2	2	2	8	$0.45	$3.60	$0.25	$2.00	$1.60						
Packer	5	5	10	5	25	$0.50	$12.50	$0.15	$3.75	$8.75						
Stay Sharp	1	2	3	4	10	$0.40	$4.00	$0.17	$1.70	$2.30						
Yellow	10	10	10	10	40	$0.25	$10.00	$0.20	$8.00	$2.00	$48.39	19.2%				
PENS																
Blue/Black	6	5	5	4	20	$0.50	$10.00	$0.31	$6.20	$3.80						
Colorful	3	6	3	8	20	$0.65	$13.00	$0.39	$7.80	$5.20						
Erasable Blue/ Black	2	2	5	5	14	$0.50	$7.00	$0.29	$4.06	$2.94						
Shimmers	8	9	8	9	34	$0.75	$25.50	$0.33	$11.22	$14.28						
Wavelengths	7	8	8	7	30	$0.50	$15.00	$0.33	$9.90	$5.10						
Gel Rollers	15	16	17	18	66	$1.10	$72.60	$0.71	$46.86	$25.74	$57.06	22.6%				
FOLDERS	8	7	8	7	30	$0.25	$7.50	$0.13	$3.90	$3.60	$3.60	1.4%				
CANDY																
Chips	21	22	23	24	90	$0.50	$45.00	$0.25	$22.50	$22.50	$22.50	8.9%				
Candy Bars	24	23	22	21	90	$0.50	$45.00	$0.25	$22.50	$22.50	$22.50	8.9%				
Gum	15	16	17	18	66	$0.50	$33.00	$0.25	$16.50	$16.50	$16.50	6.5%				
TOTALS					886		$553.30		$301.33	$251.97		$1.00				

Information and notes about bookkeeping:

Determine Staffing and Job Titles

- Assign duties according to individual strengths and/or interests
- Remember to work as a team

The age and ability of the employees may need to be taken into consideration when staffing the store for business. There are different scenarios of staffing combinations that may need to be considered. One, two, or three employees may be needed at any one time, depending on the age and abilities of the employees. School store advisors can assist by training students and by performing those tasks that may be, at first, too difficult for students to perform. See appendix E for a listing of possible job descriptions.

At the elementary level, more employees per shift may be needed to work at the same time. For example, one employee may be positioned behind the store counter to describe and retrieve products for customers. A second employee may be needed and positioned in front of the store to assist "younger customers." That employee can help younger customers count their money, if needed, and clarify which products fall within their financial means. A third employee may be needed to operate the cash box. To avoid confusion, the person working as cashier should be the only person taking money and making change.

If you have students form a line, transactions may be more orderly than chaotic. You may want to only allow two or three students at a time in front of the counter and the rest wait in line.

Even though employees of the school store have specific job titles, all the employees can still work as a team. Situations and schedules may arise where it is not possible to have specific job titles. There may be one or several employees that do several jobs to make the efficiency of the business run smoother. One does not have to be limited to specifics if it works best to do multi-tasking. For example, the bookkeeper may be a sales clerk for a day, and while working, he or she may organize the display, clean the store, and notice that supplies need to be ordered.

Information and notes about staffing and job titles

____

____

____

____

____

____

____

____

Select a Location for Your Business

- Discuss the type of location that is most suitable for the business
- Decide on a location and a time
- Get permission to use the location

Find a convenient time and place where you can position your store to conduct business. It might be best to discuss this with your building principal and/or the school store committee. An ideal location may be one that can tolerate increases in traffic and noise. The advertising staff can make sure everyone knows when and where the store is open through announcements, posters, and other types of advertising.

Regardless of who sets the hours, you may find that limiting the store's hours and days per week keeps the excitement and flexibility at a maximum. One week the store may have to be open during recess and the following week during lunch. The number of employees your store has may be a consideration when determining store hours. Students may be needed before school, at class time, during recess, during lunch, or after school.

Information and notes about selecting a location for your business:

____

____

____

____

____

____

____

____

____

____

____

____

____

____

Plan for Equipment and Supplies

- List all the equipment and supplies you will need
- Find out where you can get it
- How much does it cost?
- Check prices for each item and comparison shop
- Possibly fill out a purchase order and give it to the person in charge of purchasing

Figure 5-1

Once you have your employees, the equipment you need, know the locations where you are going to sell, and have done a little pre-business business, you may want to think about supplies.

School store supplies can fall into several categories. These categories may include essentials and teacher required items (composition books, assignment books, colored pencils, crayons, inexpensive pencils and pens, erasers, paper, etc.), novelty items ("fun", "colorful", or "cool" items that catch the students eye), food (candy, snacks, granola bars, popcorn, soda, etc.) and entrepreneurial items (silk-screened shirts, hats, buttons, etc. from other in-school makers/ businesses or local distributors).

As you make preparations to choose suppliers and a line of products, it is important to find out which products sell and at what prices. Figure 5-1 shows a popular selling pen. Surveys and questionnaires are good tools to use when determining which school store supplies students may need or want. These can be given to both staff and students. Teachers may have rules regarding the types of products that they will allow in their classrooms. This is not to say that the school store can't sell them. That is why surveys are important. It is student-selected products, subject to the approval of store advisor(s), and/or teachers that may ensure the success of your store. The results of these surveys will give you a pretty good idea of products to stock your store with. You may want to give the surveys to students, teachers, parents, or anyone else you feel may be a potential customer or person of interest. The surveys can be integrated into math and other classes. The results can be tallied, interpreted, and graphed. Related classroom activities and lesson plans are located in appendix G.

Be careful of getting stuck with some of these items when the popularity dies. It may be better to have some customers asking for more, than to have a gross of something you can't give away.

The next page has an example of a school store survey, which can be modified to meet individual needs.

Sample School Store Survey

Please complete this survey so we can make some decisions about merchandise in the school store. Put an X on the line indicating how often you think you would buy each school supply listed.

School Supplies	Never	Once in a while	Often
Calculators	_____	_____	_____
Colored pencils	_____	_____	_____
Dictionaries	_____	_____	_____
Eraser tips	_____	_____	_____
Erasers	_____	_____	_____
Computer Disks	_____	_____	_____
Folders	_____	_____	_____
Gel Pens	_____	_____	_____
Highlighters	_____	_____	_____
Kleenex Tissues	_____	_____	_____
Loose Leaf Paper	_____	_____	_____
Markers	_____	_____	_____
Note Cards	_____	_____	_____
Pencil/Pen Grips	_____	_____	_____
Pencils	_____	_____	_____
Pens	_____	_____	_____
Rulers	_____	_____	_____
School Buttons	_____	_____	_____
School Clothing	_____	_____	_____
Scissors	_____	_____	_____
Spiral Notebooks	_____	_____	_____

Please give suggestions for other school supply items, products, or services that the school store could have for the students and staff.

____

____

Where do you think the school store should be open and why? ____________________

____

When do you think the school store should be open and why?____________________

____

Additional comments about the school store.______________________________

____

____

You and your students may use the results of the survey to assist in selecting distributors or suppliers. You will likely find a wide range of items to sell. The buyer and some other employees may want to look through a school supply catalog. Some school supply suppliers offer instant interest free credit to schools. They will open an account for you and allow you to pay your bill in weekly or monthly installments. With limited funds and/or resources to cover the start-up costs of opening the store and purchasing supplies, this option may be preferred. However, their prices may be higher than those of suppliers who do not offer the installment option. Chain retailers, like Wal-Mart or Sam's Club usually have cheaper prices but don't have the "fun" or unique items like school supply companies. Also, sometimes the retail stores don't offer the "cool" things students want like the school supply companies can. The draw back of shopping at retail outlets is that it takes more time and energy than paging through a catalog. However, this may be an opportunity to do some unit pricing with the students on a field trip. Taking students on this type of shopping excursion could be fun, educational, and empowering. Additionally, they may feel an increased sense of ownership in the school store.

Regardless of where you purchase your inventory, involve the students in the process and do some unit pricing. Unit pricing can be integrated into math classes. Some mistakes may be made. They can be accepted as part of the learning process. There is a period of trial and error, so shop around and look for bargains.

Information and notes about planning for equipment and supplies:

____

____

____

____

____

____

____

____

____

____

____

____

____

Competition

- Who are your major competitors?
- What are the major strengths of each competitor?
- What are the major weaknesses of each competitor?
- Are you familiar with your competitor's products/services?
- Where are your competitors located?
- What kind if promotional activities are your competitors doing?
- What do customers say about your competitors?

The amount of competition is going to be based on the number of fundraisers in your school, the number of retail stores in your area, and the distance from your customers to these other stores. Competing with another person in the school that is trying to raise money may cause conflict. For example, if there is a candy fundraiser for a couple of weeks to raise money for band students, you may not want to sell candy during that time.

Information and notes about competition:

Pricing

Setting prices is going be different for each school and location. Some prices may only be a few pennies above cost because the same item is sold close to your school and at a low price. Some prices may be set higher because the item cannot be found in a retail store or the retail store is a greater distance from your school. You may want to ask the students what they think they would pay for an item. Whatever the situation, setting prices is going to have a trial and error period. Prices vary with supply and demand. A gel pen that can't be found in stores makes more profit than one that can be found. The pricing process is a good way to integrate social studies (supply and demand) and math (unit cost, percent increase, percent "off" sale, fraction "off" sale, etc.), and other subjects using the school store.

Also, you may need to define one unit or product of your business and your unit price. For example, if you were selling hats, one unit would be one hat. The unit price would be the selling price of one hat. If you are selling a service, the unit is usually what you charge a customer for one hour or day of the service.

Information and notes about pricing:

Advertising

The opening of your school store and new additions to your store's product line can be introduced to your market through your advertising team. Posters, PA announcements, flyers, student made videos, and handouts are some examples. It would be a great idea to promote gift certificates for merchandise from the school store. These gift certificates can be given out to friends or family as gifts, be given out for rewards, be given out for a thank you, or be given out for other incentives.

Also, an occasional sale sparks business. Different types of sales may include 10% off, ¼ off, two-for-one, and buy "this" get "that" free. Giving away merchandise with the purchase of something else is a good way to remove unwanted merchandise, especially if the merchandise has a shelf life or the season has passed. For example, if a certain type of Halloween item is ordered and not many sold, it may be a good idea to give them away when a certain amount of money is spent on other items. The discounts and sales have students do practical math calculations as a consumer, as a clerk, and can be integrated into the classroom. Other advertising ideas include:

- Plan your advertising
    - Decide where and how you will advertise your products and/or services
    - If you are using posters, decide what kind and how many of each one you want to make
    - Decide what should be included on the poster (business name, logo, location, products and/or services offered, features and customer benefits, special offers/sales, and information or catchy slogans that will make people want to buy your products and/or services)
    - Get permission to use wall space for your posters
    - If you want to do a skit to advertise your business, get permission
    - If you want to do an announcement on the public address system, get permission
    - If you are going to do live commercials, write and practice them before doing them over the intercom
- List features and benefits—The features of your products or services create customer benefits. You can advertise the benefits to raise awareness and interest in your products and services. An example of features and benefits of flavored water is: *features*; comes in an 8 oz. bottle, has one calorie, recyclable bottle: *benefits*; easy to carry, good for weight watchers, good for the environment.
- Logos (optional)—A logo is an identifying symbol for a product or business. The logo can be printed on the business's advertising to get the public into the habit of identifying the logo with the product or service.

The next two pages have examples of P.A. announcements to promote a school store.

School Store Information Announcement

Cheerfully
Rosie: "Hi Gertrude, what would you like me to do with your hair today?"

Sad
Gertrude: "I don't care."

Concerned
Rosie: "Is everything OK? You don't sound very happy."

Sad
Gertrude: "I'm OK. I'm just feeling a little yucky because I can't think of anything to get my grandkids for Valentine's Day."

Comforting
Rosie: "Really. My kids told me that the school store at their school has all kinds of neat things that kids like, and at a low price."

Surprised
Gertrude: "No kidding. What kinds of things?"

Excited
Rosie: "Oh, like gel pens, stickers, smelly markers, candy, soda, shirts, and all kinds of stuff."

Relieved
Gertrude: "Wow. Thanks. But, where and when is it open?"

Friendly
Rosie: "It's open every Thursday from 11:30am to 12:30pm in the cafeteria at Henry & Margaret Junior High School."

Thankful
Gertrude: "Thank you for the great suggestion and information."

Cheerfully
Rosie: "You're welcome."

Excited
Gertrude: "Hey, I don't want to embarrass the kids when I go to their school. So, how about giving me some hot pink hair coloring, and spike it?"

Amazed
Rosie: "WHAT?"

School Store Service Announcement

Brittney: "Hi. Can I help you?"

Amanda: "Yes. I would like to buy a card."

Alyssa: "Me too. I would like to buy a birthday card for my mom, and I was wondering if you know how I could send it to her so it's a surprise. If I try mailing it from home, she might find out and I really want it to be a surprise."

Brittney: "The school store has a mailing service and we would be happy to mail it for you."

Amanda: "Really. How much does it cost?"

Brittney: "Just fifty cents to mail a card anywhere in the United States."

Alyssa: "How much will it cost to buy a card and have you mail it for me?"

Brittney: "The card is fifty cents and so is the mailing service. If you want both, the total is one dollar."

Amanda: "Cool. I'll take both. Thanks."

Alyssa: "Me too. Thank you."

Brittney: "And thank you for shopping at the school store."

Brittney, Amanda, and Alyssa: "BYE."

Information and notes about advertising:

____

____

____

____

____

____

____

____

____

____

Funds Needed to Start Business

One of the most important things to do before attempting to finance your business is to estimate how much money you will need. To do that, you may want to determine:

- Start-up costs—Start-up costs are the total cost of items you will need to purchase to make your first sale.
- Cost of goods sold—Cost of goods sold is the cost, including tax, of the product or service that you are selling. For example, if you pay $9.99 plus tax for a pack of 10 gel pens, your cost to sell those pens is $9.99 + $.50(tax) = $10.49, or $1.05 per pen.
- Operating costs—Operating costs include items such as utilities, interest, and other costs needed to operate the business. By adding them up and subtracting them from your gross profit, you can pinpoint your net profit (what you get to keep). Operating costs include fixed and variable costs. Fixed costs are costs that do not change with the amount of sales your business makes. Rent is a fixed cost. Variable costs are costs that change based on the number of units sold. Therefore, start-up costs + cost of goods sold + operating costs (fixed & variable) = funds needed to start business.

Information and notes about funds needed to start your business:

___

___

___

___

___

___

___

___

___

___

___

APPENDIX B
APPLICATIONS, CHECKLISTS, AND TESTS

School Store Employment Application (Elementary)

School Store Employment Application (Junior High)

Application Checklist

Interview Checklist

Interview Test

SCHOOL STORE EMPLOYMENT APPLICATION

(Elementary)

PERSONAL INFORMATION

Name____

(First and Last Name)

Age_____Grade____Date___________

Position Applying For (may be more than one)____________________________

WORK HISTORY

List Previous Work Experience (include family chores)

Description of Work Experience

____

Description of Work Experience

____

Description of Work Experience

____

REFERENCES

Recommendations: Ask an adult who knows you well to tell why you should be a school store employee (parent, grandparent, aunt/uncle, teacher, neighbor, etc).

____

____

____

Why should you be hired for this position? ________________________________

____

The above information is true and accurate to the best of my knowledge.

______________________________ ______________

Signature Date

SCHOOL STORE EMPLOYMENT APPLICATION

(Junior High)

PERSONAL INFORMATION

Name____

(First and Last Name)

Age_____Grade____Date___________

Position Applying For (may be more than one)______________________________

WORK HISTORY

List Previous Work Experience (include family chores)

Description of Work Experience

____

____

Description of Work Experience

____

____

Description of Work Experience

____

____

REFERENCES

<u>Recommendations</u>: Ask an adult who knows you well to tell why you should be a school store employee (parent, grandparent, aunt/uncle, teacher, neighbor, etc).

____

____

____

____

Please answer the following questions:

Why do you wish to work at the school store? ________________________________

____

____

Why should you be hired for the position/s which you are applying for? ______________

____

____

What experience do you have in the position/s that you are applying for? _____________

____

____

Why do you think you would be a good school store employee? ________________

____

What do you hope to learn? ____

____

What skills do you wish to acquire? ___________________________________

____

The above information is true and accurate to the best of my knowledge.

______________________________ ________________

Signature Date

APPLICATION CHECKLIST

	YES	NO
Information has been placed on the correct lines	_____	_____
All information items have been completed	_____	_____
All words have been spelled correctly	_____	_____
Forms of response are as specified (e.g. printed in ink)	_____	_____
Application has been filled out neatly	_____	_____
Job for which application is made is specified	_____	_____
Applicant has signed application	_____	_____

Additional Comments:

____

____

____

____

____

____

____

____

____

____

____

____

INTERVIEW CHECKLIST

	YES	NO
Was on time	____	____
Was well groomed/appropriately dressed	____	____
Responded appropriately to direction from interviewer	____	____
Responses were free of excessive emotionalism	____	____
Responses were complete	____	____
Gave two or more relevant facts about self	____	____
Avoided slang or street expressions during interview	____	____
Maintained good eye contact with interviewer	____	____
Maintained a friendly manner	____	____

Additional Comments:

____

____

____

____

____

____

____

____

____

____

____

INTERVIEW TEST

Name:_________________________________Date:___________________

READ EACH QUESTION CAREFULLY. MAKE ONLY ONE SELECTION OF THE CHOICES LISTED AND CIRCLE THE APPROPRIATE LETTER.

1. The job interview takes place between you and the . . .
   a. person in charge of hiring.
   b. sales manager.
   c. company president.
   d. person who had the job last.

2. In job interviews, employers may ask questions about . . .
   a. past jobs.
   b. personal interests.
   c. education.
   d. all of the above.

3. If you had a job interview at 9:00 A.M., you should . . .
   a. be a little late because interviews never start on time.
   b. get there exactly at 9:00 A.M.
   c. get there 5 to 10 minutes early.
   d. get there at 8:00 A.M. to be the first in line.

4. When you go to the job interview, you should . . .
   a. dress neatly in clean, conservative clothes.
   b. wear the uniform you would be wearing at this place of business.
   c. put on anything handy.
   d. wear the fanciest clothes you have.

5. In a job interview it is O.K. to ask questions about . . .
   a. the duties you will have.
   b. the type of work performed at this place of business.
   c. your hours, salary, and possible benefits.
   d. all of the above.

6. Bill has a job interview with a private security agency he knows little about. He should . . .
   a. learn about the company before the interview and find out what types of skills are needed.
   b. dress up for the interview and not worry about the history of the company.
   c. explain during the interview that he does not know much about the company, but he would sure like to learn.
   d. wait until the interview and see what happens.

7. Jeannie wants to be at her interview on time so she asks her friend Dave to give her a ride. Dave should . . .
   a. give her a ride to the interview, but stay outside.
   b. give her a ride and go into the interview with her because she is afraid.
   c. give her a ride and ask if he can go into the interview and watch.
   d. not give her a ride because it does not matter if she is there on time.

8. At a job interview, it's good practice to spend the most time discussing . . .
   a. wages and salary.
   b. frequency of raises.
   c. company fringe benefits.
   d. your qualifications for the job.

9. After the job interview is over you should . . .
   a. thank the interviewer for his/her time.
   b. ask if they will contact you about their decision.
   c. ask when a decision will be made.
   d. any of the above.

10. At the end of a job interview, if the employer has not said anything about getting the job, you should . . .
   a. figure you blew it.
   b. wait a few days, then forget about it.
   c. ask when they will be making their decision.
   d. ask what went wrong and see if you can get another interview.

11. The main purpose of a job interview is to . . .
   a. make sure that all forms have been filled out.
   b. find out about an employee's attitudes, behavior, and interest in the job.
   c. introduce employees to company rules.
   d. discuss salary and fringe benefits.

12. Under what conditions is it O.K. to wear older or sloppy clothes to an interview?
   a. When the working conditions are such that all employees wear old clothes to work everyday.
   b. When the interview is for a job at an auto repair shop.
   c. When you are applying for a job at a place where the building is under construction.
   d. Never.

13. Carol, age 17, is applying for her first job. The interviewer surprises her by asking, "What do you hope to be doing in 10 years for now?" Carol's best answer would be . . .
   a. "I hope that I will be married and will not have to work."
   b. "Could we come back to that question later?"
   c. "I hope that I will be making a lot of money and driving a sports car."
   d. "I hope to be working at a job which is challenging me."

14. Mr. Thompson has been out of work for 3 months. Now he has a lot of bills he cannot pay. He thinks that he would take almost any job just to put food on the table. An interviewer asks him, "Why do you want to work for our company?" Mr. Thompson should answer . . .
   a. "I think that I could do a good job here."
   b. "One company is as good as another."
   c. "I don't care where I work. I will take any job just to put food on the table."
   d. "I don't know."

15. Which of the following would be the best activity for Chris to do to prepare for a job interview?
    a. Try on eye-catching jewelry.
    b. Practice calling the interviewer by her last name.
    c. Pick out an impressive book to carry to the interview.
    d. Practice answering questions about past jobs and experiences.

Answer Key: 1.A, 2.D, 3.C, 4.A, 5.D, 6.A, 7.A, 8.D, 9.D, 10.C, 11.B, 12.D, 13.D, 14.A, 15.D

APPENDIX C

GENERAL GUIDELINES FOR SCHOOL STORE EMPLOYEES

1. Work as a team. You can help each other.
2. Never eat snacks or drink soda while you are working. The products could get sticky or dirty.
3. Wear clean appropriate clothing and be properly groomed while you are working (hair combed, clean hands and fingernails, etc.).
4. Keep the store supplies and the money locked up when not in use.
5. Be polite to all customers.
6. Keep the store neat and straightened.
7. Use a piece of paper and a pencil or a calculator to add up items whenever you have a lot and can't do the math in your head.
8. Count back change from all sales. Start with the total price of the item(s). This helps you and the customers know that the change is correct.
9. Don't joke with a customer's money.
10. Don't allow customers to loiter or joke with you.
11. Don't play with items in the store.
12. Don't use items from the store unless you have purchased them. Have another store employee make the sale and take your money.
13. Never leave the store unattended.
14. Never give credit to customers without the manager's approval. All sales are cash, unless the manager says otherwise; even if they are short a penny.
15. Don't talk with your friends while working at the store.
16. Don't let anyone fluster or confuse you. If they do, stop the sale at that point and start over.
17. Don't have money or store items unattended or where people may be able to take them.
18. Don't ever put money from sold items in your pocket for self-keeping. Stealing money or items from the store is a crime.
19. Don't leave money from sold items in the store. Deposit it immediately or secure it in a safe place.
20. Don't be tardy. Report to work on time.
21. Stay calm. Use common sense. When in doubt, ask for help.

Figure 5-2

Figure 5-2 shows a guideline for employees that work with food items.

APPENDIX D

EMPLOYABILITY SKILLS AND ATTITUDES

Components of Employability Skills and Attitudes

- The K-12 curriculum includes specific career education units, lessons, objectives, and evaluation criteria emphasizing employability skills and attitudes
- Work experience methodologies emphasizing employability skills and attitudes
- A developmental guidance model can be used to develop employment skills and attitudes
- Private sector/school partnerships are utilized to insure instruction in employment skills and attitudes
- The teaching of employability skills and attitudes is part of both the vocational and general curriculum
- The work ethic is integrated into total school policies and practices

Competencies of Employability Skills and Attitudes

Work Ethic

- Work well without supervision
- Exhibit reliability and dependability
- Accept responsibility
- Work beyond normal hours when needed
- Show pride in work
- Accept responsibility for own behavior
- Show initiative
- Conduct self in a calm and controlled manner
- Demonstrate maturity in thought, actions, and deeds
- Exhibit patience
- Manage time efficiently and effectively
- Display appropriate assertiveness
- Evaluate own work

Commitment

- Observe all organizational policies
- Demonstrate interest and enthusiasm in the job
- Consider work as more than a job
- Exhibit loyalty to the organization and its employees
- Display a desire to improve
- Give best effort consistently and strive to please
- Show concern for future career with the organization
- Understand the world of work and basic economic concepts

Communication

- Question appropriately
- Notify supervisors of absences and reasons for absences
- Seek help when needed
- Demonstrate clear effective written and oral communication skills
- Demonstrate good listening and responding techniques
- Develop telephone skills

Interpersonal Relationships

- Work well with peers
- Accept authority and supervision; work effectively with supervisor
- Accept constructive criticism
- Work as a team member
- Display a friendly and cooperative spirit
- Accept assignments pleasantly
- Demonstrate tactfulness in difficult situations
- Become aware of and accepting of cultural differences
- Respect the rights and property of others
- Display leadership qualities
- Identify varying management styles
- Understand self and need to accept value systems of others

Responsibility

- Organize work and manage time efficiently
- Exhibit accuracy, precision, and neatness in work and work habits
- Demonstrate ability to complete assignments in a timely manner
- Follow oral, visual, written, and multi-step directions
- Display care for tools and materials
- Strive to improve job performance
- Seek new assignments when time permits
- Understand employer expectations

Job Seeking and Job Getting Skills

- Become aware of creative potential
- Utilize creative ability in on-the-job situations
- Prepare job applications and resumes
- Conduct career/job search
- Develop job application letters
- Demonstrate effective interviewing skills
- Display understanding of benefits and payroll procedures

Reasoning and Problem Solving
- Display flexibility
- Integrate creative and innovative ideas
- Synthesize and process job components
- Adapt to changing demands of the job
- Organize work and manage time efficiently
- Reason and make objective judgments
- Understand rules and procedures
- Apply basic skills

Health and Safety Habits
- Observe safety rules
- Maintain a good work pace and production rate
- Practice good personal hygiene
- Dress in a well-groomed and appropriate manner
- Recognize stress-related situations and deal with them effectively
- Develop physical stamina and tolerance for the kind of work being done
- Maintain good personal health

Personal Attributes
- Develop good self esteem and a positive self image
- Define personal and professional goals
- Demonstrate emotional stability
- Exhibit positive attitudes
- Demonstrate self motivation and self management
- Develop an understanding of motivation for work
- Exhibit self confidence and self awareness
- Display honesty in personal and work situations

Reprinted/excerpted from Education For Employment with permission from the Wisconsin Department of Public Instruction, 125 South Webster Street, Madison, WI 53702.

Reference 1

Regardless of where or when a business survey is conducted, the most frequent response is that employees need employability skills. Employability skills and attitudes refer to the skills and attitudes needed to obtain and retain general employment. The ability to communicate, get along with others, work ethic, and accuracy are some examples. In the Madison, Wisconsin area, a random survey [by Vicki A. Poole, "Work Experience Program Can Help Develop Human Relation Skills," *Business Education Forum,* January 1985, pp. 9-10. and "Business Finds Grads Unskilled," Capital Times (Madison, WI), June 27, 1984, p.1], of 205 employers was conducted to determine the technical skills and personal characteristics employers felt were most important for beginning employees. Of the 15 technical skills listed, only four were considered either important or very important by 90 percent or more of the employers. However, of the 15 personal characteristics listed, 12 were considered either important or very important by 90 percent or more of the employers. These 12 personal characteristics include: ability to work with others, ability to follow directions, confidence, cooperation, dependability, efficiency, initiative, judgment, neatness, conduct, produces quality work, and punctuality.

The following are some comments from employers.
"Unfortunately, many of the potential employees possessing ability and potential fail to make the most of their skills because they lack positive personal characteristics—cooperation, dependability, and a willingness to work."

"Employees need to learn more about communicating with co-workers."

"I feel students should be taught to come to work on time and the importance of giving the employer a full day's work."

"I think schools should instill in their students how important it is to be conscientious about their work quality and let them know that the world does not owe them a living"

On the national level, a business financed research organization surveyed about 500 human resources and public affairs executives. Their report found that recent high school graduates have trouble following orders, communicate poorly, and have poor work attitudes. One respondent said, "Business can teach new hires how to add if they have to, but they can't teach them to take their jobs seriously." A utility executive said there is a "basic problem convincing the high school graduates that there is an ethic of responsibility in the work place that requires that you show up for work."

Reference 2

The two greatest concerns of employers today are finding good workers and training them. The difference between the skills needed on the job and those possessed by applicants, sometimes called the skills-gap, is of real concern to human resource managers and business owners looking to hire competent employees. While employers would prefer to hire people who are trained and ready to go to work, they are usually willing to provide the specialized, job-specific training necessary for those lacking such skills. Most discussions concerning today's workforce eventually turn to employability skills. Finding workers who have employability or job readiness skills that help them fit into and remain in the work environment is a real problem. Employers need reliable, responsible workers who can solve problems and who have the social skills and attitudes to work together with other workers. Creativity, once a trait avoided by employers who used a cookie cutter system, is now prized among employers who are trying to create the empowered, high performance workforce needed for competitiveness in today's marketplace. Employees with these skills are in demand and are considered valuable human capital assets to companies. Employability skills are those basic skills necessary for getting, keeping, and doing well on a job. These are the skills, attitudes and actions that enable workers to get along with their fellow workers and supervisors and to make sound, critical decisions. Unlike occupational or technical skills, employability skills are generic in nature rather than job specific and cut across all industry types, business sizes, and job levels from the entry-level worker to the senior-most position. What specifically are those skills, attitudes and actions, i.e., employability skills, necessary for getting, keeping, and doing well on a job? Employability skills, while categorized in many different ways, are generally divided into three skill sets:

- basic academic skills (reading, writing, science, math, oral communication, listening)
- higher-order thinking skills (learning, reasoning, thinking, creatively, decisions making, problem solving)
- personal qualities (responsible self confidence, self control, social skills, honest, have integrity, adaptable and flexible, team spirit, punctual and efficient, self directed, good work attitude, well groomed, cooperative, self motivated, self management)

Although the academic skill level required by some entry-level jobs may be low, basic academic skills are still essential for high job performance. Ideally, new hires will have the ability and will want to learn. They also need the ability to listen to and read instructions and then to carry out those instructions. When asked for information, these individuals should be able to respond appropriately both orally and in writing, including recording and relaying information. Reading ability includes comprehending what has been read and using a variety of written materials, including graphs, charts, tables and displays. Entry level employees also need the ability to complete basic math computations accurately. Perhaps even more important to job success than having good basic academic skills, is having good higher-order thinking skills. The ability to think, reason, and make sound decisions is crucial for employees desiring to do well and advance. A person who can think critically, act logically, and evaluate situations to make decisions and solve problems, is a valuable asset. Application of higher order thinking skills in the use of technology, instruments, tools and information systems takes these higher order skills to a new level making the employee even more valuable. Employers will usually try to help valued employees seek and get more advanced training, thus widening the gap between those with higher order skills and those possessing basic academic skills alone.

If basic academic skills and higher order thinking skills are so important, why then are employers deeply concerned with personal skills? Because in most jobs, it is difficult to utilize workers effectively who lack personal skills. Entry-level employees with good personal skills have confidence in themselves and deal with others honestly and openly, displaying respect for themselves, their co-workers, and their supervisors regardless of other people's diversity and individual differences. They view themselves as a part of a team and are willing to work within the culture of the group. They have a positive attitude and take the initiative to learn new things to get the job done. Rather than blaming others when things go wrong, they are accountable for their actions. They also have the ability to set goals and priorities in their work and personal lives so that resources of time, money and other resources may be conserved and managed. These individuals practice good personal habits, come to work as scheduled, on time and dressed appropriately, and are agreeable to change when necessary. Failure to equip young people with the job readiness skills critical to job success is equivalent to placing employability barriers in their path. Allowing students to graduate with these deficiencies has far reaching implications. There are ways; however, these deficiencies may be corrected. For example:

- Employability skills are teachable skills and may be taught in both school and employment settings. Goals and objectives for teaching employability skills should be set. Instruction should be designed to ensure those goals and objectives are reached.
- Parents need to be involved in goal setting and modeling behavior for in-school youth.
- Teach employability skills using a democratic approach so that students' awareness of values, attitudes, and worker responsibilities is increased.
- Supervisors, trainers and teachers should set good examples of the desired behavior.
- Students should have the opportunity to observe the type of work place behavior that is being required of them.
- When possible, classrooms should replicate the features of real work settings.
- Set and communicate high expectations and hold students responsible for their behavior.
- Teach, don't tell. Teachers and trainers tend to be most effective when they assume the role of coach or facilitator.

It is often said that it is too late to teach values after a child has reached or completed high school; that their personality is set and nothing can change it. That is not true. It is, fortunately, never too late. Change may be difficult, but it can be done. Teaching of values should begin in the home as a child, be continued through development to adulthood, and reinforced as an adult. If good behavior is reinforced and good role models are presented, people can change for the better. Good habits can be acquired. Employers, schools and parents should remember that you get the behavior you reward and model.

Excerped from http://www.aces.edu/crd/workforce/publications/employability-skills.
Needleman, E. C. (1995). *Preparing Youth for Employable Futures.* Washington, DC: National 4-H Council Secretary's Commission on Achieving Necessary Skills (no date). *Skills and Tasks for Jobs.* A SCANS Report for America 2000. Washington, DC: U.S. Department of Labor.

APPENDIX E

JOB DESCRIPTIONS

Advertising Associates:

- Promote the goods and services of the store through posters, ads, and airtime (school announcements)
- Negotiate with building principals and/or other faculty to use wall space and airtime for advertising
- Devise campaigns to sell slow moving merchandise

Bookkeeping Associates:

- Maintain records of accounts and financial transactions for the school store

Buying Associates:

- Purchase merchandise for sale/resale at the school store
- Search catalogs, the internet, and retail outlets for items for the store that students may like

Receiving/Inventory Control Associates:

- Keep records on all incoming shipments from the store's suppliers
- Check incoming shipments against the original orders and unpack/examine items for damages and/or shortages
- Responsible for store inventories

Sales Associates:

- Wait on customers
- Make change
- Help smaller kids count their money and select products
- Assist customers with the selection and purchase of products
- Describe the features of the products, demonstrate how the products work, or show the different varieties of products
- Sales workers may also stock shelves, take inventory, price products, and clean

Managing Associates:

- Supervise all school store employees
- Solve problems and complaints
- Help teach other employees
- Help out as needed

The managing associates oversee the operation of the store and report to the advisors/coordinators on a regular basis. For example, they may check the store and make sure advertising is current and correct price sheets are available. They may see if change is available for the day's business, make sure inventories are conducted on a regular basis, reorder items as needed, plan and prepare work schedules, assign specific duties, help set pricing, and coordinate sales promotions. The manager may be directly or indirectly involved with everything relating to the store. Good judgment, leadership skills, and the ability to work well with people are some characteristics of a successful managing associate.

APPENDIX F

EVALUATIONS AND TESTS

Worker Maturity Employee Performance Self Evaluation (Elementary)

Worker Maturity Employee Performance Teacher Evaluation (Elementary)

Worker Maturity Employee Performance Self Evaluation (Junior High)

Worker Maturity Employee Performance Teacher Evaluation (Junior High)

Worker Maturity Test

Understanding Labor Market Information Test

WORKER MATURITY
EMPLOYEE PERFORMANCE SELF EVALUATION
(Elementary)

Name________________________________JobDescription________________________

Directions: Circle the rating for each work attitude you think applies to you.

Work Attitude	Rating		
I am responsible	Good	OK	Improve
I am on time	Good	OK	Improve
I listen carefully	Good	OK	Improve
I do my best	Good	OK	Improve
I am happy	Good	OK	Improve
I work well with others	Good	OK	Improve
I am honest	Good	OK	Improve
I am organized	Good	OK	Improve

Other comments about yourself:

____

____

____

____

____

____

WORKER MATURITY
EMPLOYEE PERFORMANCE TEACHER EVALUATION
(Elementary)

Name__________________________________JobDescription__________________________

Directions: Circle the rating for each work attitude you think applies to your employee.

Work Attitude	Rating		
Employee is responsible	Good	OK	Improve
Employee is on time	Good	OK	Improve
Employee listens carefully	Good	OK	Improve
Employee does their best	Good	OK	Improve
Employee is happy	Good	OK	Improve
Employee works well with others	Good	OK	Improve
Employee is honest	Good	OK	Improve
Employee is organized	Good	OK	Improve

Other comments about the employee:

____

____

____

____

____

____

____

WORKER MATURITY
EMPLOYEE PERFORMANCE SELF EVALUATION
(Junior High)

Name____Job Description___________________

Place an "X" in the appropriate space for each characteristic you think applies to you. Excellent = A; Above Average = B; Average = C; Poor = D; F = Does not meet minimum expectation; N/A = Not Available

Characteristic	A	B	C	D	F	N/A
I demonstrate a willingness to learn	__	__	__	__	__	__
I exhibit acceptable personal grooming	__	__	__	__	__	__
I report to work on time	__	__	__	__	__	__
I apply myself to the job	__	__	__	__	__	__
I adapt to new situations	__	__	__	__	__	__
I initiate work without supervision	__	__	__	__	__	__
I do my job satisfactorily	__	__	__	__	__	__
I possess emotional stability	__	__	__	__	__	__
I show self-confidence	__	__	__	__	__	__
I follow directions	__	__	__	__	__	__
I accept criticism	__	__	__	__	__	__
I exhibit the ability to work with others	__	__	__	__	__	__
I work safely	__	__	__	__	__	__
I work above and beyond demands	__	__	__	__	__	__

Average Grade_____

Other comments about yourself:

____

____

____

____

WORKER MATURITY
EMPLOYEE PERFORMANCE TEACHER EVALUATION
(Junior High)

Name____Job Description__________________

Place an "X" in the appropriate space for each characteristic you think applies to your empleyee.
Excellent = A; Above Average = B; Average = C; Poor = D; F = Does not meet minimum expectation; N/A = Not Available

Characteristic	A	B	C	D	F	N/A
Employee demonstrates a willingness to learn	__	__	__	__	__	__
Employee exhibits acceptable personal grooming	__	__	__	__	__	__
Employee reports to work on time	__	__	__	__	__	__
Employee applies self to the job	__	__	__	__	__	__
Employee adapts to new situations	__	__	__	__	__	__
Employee initiates work without supervision	__	__	__	__	__	__
Employee does the job satisfactorily	__	__	__	__	__	__
Employee possesses emotional stability	__	__	__	__	__	__
Employee shows self-confidence	__	__	__	__	__	__
Employee follows directions	__	__	__	__	__	__
Employee accepts criticism	__	__	__	__	__	__
Employee exhibits ability to work with others	__	__	__	__	__	__
Employee works safely	__	__	__	__	__	__
Employee works above and beyond demands	__	__	__	__	__	__

Average Grade_____

Other comments about the employee:

____

____

____

____

WORKER MATURITY TEST

Name:____________________Date:_____________

READ EACH QUESTION CAREFULLY. MAKE ONLY ONE SELECTION OF THE CHOICES LISTED AND CIRCLE THE APPROPRIATE LETTER.

1. On your job you have to wear steel-plated safety shoes to protect your feet. You don't like to wear them because they are very heavy. What should you do?
   a. Wear regular shoes that look like the safety shoes.
   b. Tell your boss that you don't like them and won't wear them.
   c. Refuse to work unless they let you wear what you want.
   d. Try to get used to the safety shoes so you can wear them at work.

2. For the last month you have been required to work overtime, and you're not very happy. You should . . .
   a. quit right away.
   b. call in sick once in a while.
   c. talk to your supervisor to see how long this may go on.
   d. talk to the president of the company.

3. Pete overslept. He knows that he is going to be over an hour late for work. The best thing for him to do is to . . .
   a. not worry about it. Everyone is late once in a while.
   b. just take his time and figure out what to say when he gets to work.
   c. take the whole day off because it's easier than explaining that he overslept.
   d. call the office and tell them that he overslept and will be late.

4. Cooperation on the job demands that each worker . . .
   a. help out another worker when it's necessary to get the job done.
   b. always tell others ways to do their job better.
   c. tell the supervisor any time other employees have arguments or make mistakes.
   d. minds their own business and doesn't talk to others until after work.

5. Betsy has been asked to do a dull and dirty job at the dime store. She should . . .
   a. do a poor job so the boss won't assign her this kind of work again.
   b. complain about the assignment.
   c. inform her supervisor that she feels ill.
   d. get the job done as soon as she can.

6. If your job is scheduled to start at 8:00A.M, you should . . .
   a. show up at 7:OOA.M.
   b. be no more than 10 minutes late.
   c. be working at 8:00 A.M.
   d. walk in the door at 8:OO A.M.

7. If you feel too ill to go to work, you should . . .
   a. call and let someone know you won't be in.
   b. tell your boss why you were out and when you are feeling better.
   c. not worry about it. Everyone gets sick once in a while.
   d. call when you happen to think about it.

8. To get along with co-workers you should . . .
   a. tell them what you really think of them, good or bad.
   b. go out with them after work a few times each week.
   c. listen to what they have to say and respond in a friendly way.
   d. all of the above

9. Most employers expect new workers to . . .
   a. show interest in what they are working on.
   b. work very carefully, not going too fast at first, because they are learning.
   c. ask fellow workers if they have questions about the job.
   d. all of the above.

10. What does a "job probation period" mean?
    a. Trial or try-out period when one begins a new job
    b. Overtime wages
    c. A warning time
    d. All of the above

11. Most employers expect their workers to . . .
    a. take a few days off every couple of weeks.
    b. use all of their sick days each year.
    c. come to work every day, even when they are sick.
    d. come to work every day, unless they are sick.

12. Alex's boss says that Alex has a "positive attitude" about work. This means that Alex . . .
    a. is not a very reliable worker.
    b. does not have to follow company rules because he is smart.
    c. can ask for more time off because the boss likes him.
    d. is a good, reliable worker who can be counted on to get the job done.

13. Which of these is proper dress for a male salesperson in a department store?
    a. Blue jeans and a faded T-shirt
    b. A nice pair of dress pants and a coordinating shirt and tie
    c. Shorts and a sweatshirt
    d. Whatever happens to be clean

ANSWER QUESTIONS 14 AND 15 BASED ON THE SITUATION DESCRIBED

Bob's first day at the Burgerhouse began during the lunch hour. Mr. Ray, the boss, showed Bob how to make fries and fix colas. He said, "OK Bob take over." Bob started making cola orders and then had to make some orders of fries. When the fries ran out, he had to make more, but he forgot how many minutes to cook them. Bob left the fries in the deep fryer too long and they came out burned. Orders began "backing up". Then Mr. Ray told Bob to get out of the way if he couldn't do things right.

14. Bob should have . . .
    a. told Mr. Ray that he did not want to make fries.
    b. asked another worker how long to cook the fries.
    c. told another worker to make the fries because he was making colas.
    d. quit right away because he made a mistake.
15. In the example above, Bob is mad at his boss. He should talk to him and say . . .

a. "I forgot how long to cook the fries. Next time I will ask someone for help"
b. "If you do not like me, get someone else to do the job"
c. "Don't get mad at me, I was just doing what you told me to do"
d. "You should have told me how long to cook the fries"

Answer Key: 1.D, 2.C, 3.D, 4.A, 5.D, 6.C, 7.B, 8.C, 9.D, 10.A, 11.D, 12.D, 13.B, 14.B, 15.A

UNDERSTANDING LABOR MARKET INFORMATION TEST

Name:____Date___________________

READ EACH QUESTION CAREFULLY. MAKE ONLY ONE SELECTION OF THE CHOICES LISTED AND CIRCLE THE APPROPRIATE LETTER

1. Where would you look in the newspaper to find the list of job openings for your area?
   a. The local news section
   b. The entertainment and travel section
   c. The classified ads section
   d. The sports and investment section

2. When you find a job listing in the want ads which interests you, you should . . .
   a. call immediately no matter what the ad says.
   b. apply in person in the next two weeks.
   c. send in your resume no matter what the ad says.
   d. read the ad carefully and do exactly what it tells you to do.

3. Which of the following best describes the advantages of using the Workforce Development Center?
   a. No cost; provides job counseling; some skills testing; listings of some job openings
   b. No forms to fill out; cost based on ability to pay
   c. No crowds; provides contact with all possible employers in the area
   d. No cost; no forms to fill out; used by all employers

4. Which sources of job information should you consider when hunting for a job?
   a. Family and friends
   b. Workforce Development Center
   c. Non-profit agencies
   d. All of the above

5. Which method of finding a job is the best?
   a. Applying for jobs found in the newspaper
   b. Registering at the Workforce Development Center
   c. Asking friends and relatives to watch for job openings
   d. All of the above

6. The term "Federal Minimum Wage" means . . .
   a. earning $8.00 per hour.
   b. the starting pay in every position.
   c. the standard set by the federal government for the lowest allowable wage.
   d. $1.00 per hour, the lowest wage an employee may legally earn.

7. When you go directly to a company or business to apply for a job, you should . . .
   a. ask to see the personnel manager.
   b. demand an interview.
   c. talk with other employees.
   d. ask for the boss.

8. You are looking for a job. As you walk down the street you see a "Help Wanted" sign in a store window. The best thing to do is . . .
   a. go right home and call the store manager.
   b. go right in and apply/inquire about the job.
   c. write a letter of application to the owner.
   d. forget it, its probably filled.

9. In a newspaper, where would you expect to find a listing for a part-time job as a cook?
   a. In the classified section under "cook"
   b. In the Entertainment section
   c. Under "miscellaneous"
   d. Under "$100 Jobs"

USE THIS INFORMATION TO ANSWER QUESTIONS 10-13

CLASSIFIED ADS:

Food Service General Worker: We are looking for a part-time individual to work flexible hours. This versatile individual will be doing kitchen duties. Free meals and uniforms. Apply in person to:

AA Food Service,
222 Cherry Ln.,
Foodsville, NC
Ask for Jack Spratt

Telephone Sales: Part-time, full time. Our office. Must call 273-2398.

10. How should you apply for the "Telephone Sales' job listed above?
    a. By person
    b. By phone
    c. By mail
    d. Send resume

11. What is the main skill needed for the "Food Service" job listed above?
    a. General kitchen duties
    b. Buffet setup
    c. Versatility
    d. All of the above

12. How would you apply for the "Food Service" job listed above?
    a. Send resume
    b. Apply in person
    c. Call for an appointment
    d. Fax resume

13. What are the benefits offered in the "Food Service" job listed above?
    a. Pension plan
    b. Two-week paid vacation
    c. Full-time work
    d. None of the above

Answer Key: 1.C, 2.D, 3.A, 4.D, 5.D, 6.C, 7.A, 8.B, 9.A, 10.B, 11.C, 12.B, 13.D

APPENDIX G
CLASSROOM ACTIVITIES

INTRODUCTION

The following classroom activities include math and writing.

Math

The math activities are ordered from the elementary level to the junior high level. Each math activity describes the grade/s, gives an overview of the activity, tells the objectives, lists the performance standards achieved with the activity, lists materials needed (if any), and describes the procedure for the activity. These activities can be modified to meet your scope, goals, or age of your students. The math activity's "Performance Standards" sections show which parts of Wisconsin's Department of Public Instruction performance standards can be achieved for math, depending on your scope and goals. These standards can be used as a template to develop, justify, facilitate, and/or achieve state standards in your state using your school store. The lesson activities that follow are:

Measurement Involving Money (Grades Kindergarten and up/Math)
Time to Shop (Grades 2 and up/Math)
Measurement Involving Length and Weight (Grades 3 and up/Math)
Number Operations and Relations Involving Money (Grades 3 and up/Math)
Interpreting Data (Grades 4 and up/Math)
Spreadsheet and Graphing Activity (Grades 5 and up/Math/Technology Education)
Analyzing Cost, Profit, and Revenue of a School Store (Grades 6 and up/Math)
Brainteasers (Kindergarten and up)

Writing

Depending on your scope and goals, the writing activities pertain to concepts of employment or operating a school store. The topics include being a good employee, diversity in the workplace, customer service, working together, goal setting, work commitment, dealing with anger, and giving advice. These essay topics can be modified to meet your scope, goals, and age of your students. These essays may be timed or untimed and written or typed. If the essays are written or typed, the essays may be exchanged between students. Then, the students can critique and/or make revisions of each others essays. The essays can then be re-written after peer critique. Or, the essays can be written or typed and critiqued by the teacher.

These writing activities don't necessarily have to be written or typed. These activities can be communicated orally. Students can listen, comprehend, and effectively discuss ideas and opinions of the presenter's essay topic.

The Wisconsin performance standards that may be achieved integrating the school store essay topics are:

B.4.1 Create or produce writing to communicate with different audiences for a variety of purposes.

- Write nonfiction and technical pieces (summaries, messages, informational essays, basic directions, instructions, simple reports) that convey essential details and facts and provide accurate representations of events and sequences
- Write in a variety of situations (timed and untimed, at school and at home) and adapt strategies, such as revision and the use of reference materials, to the situation
- Use a variety of writing technologies, including pen and paper as well as computers
- Write for a variety of readers, including peers, teachers, and other adults, adapting content, style, and structure to audience and situation

B.4.2 Plan, revise, edit, and publish clear and effective writing.

- Produce multiple drafts, including finished pieces, that demonstrate the capacity to generate, focus, and organize ideas and to revise the language, organization, and content of successive drafts in order to fulfill a specific purpose for communicating with a specific audience
- Explain the extent and reasons for revision in conference with a teacher
- Given a writing assignment to be completed in a limited amount of time, produce a well developed, well organized, and effective response in correct English and an appropriate voice

B.8.1 Create or produce writing to communicate with different audiences for a variety of purposes.

- Write a persuasive piece (such as a letter to a specific person or a script promoting a particular product) that includes a clear position, a discernible tone, and a coherent argument with reliable evidence
- Use a variety of writing technologies including pen and paper as well as computers
- Write for a variety of readers, including peers, teachers, and other adults, adapting content, style, and structure to audience and situation

B.8.2 Plan, revise, edit, and publish clear and effective writing.

- Produce multiple drafts, including finished pieces, that demonstrate the capacity to generate, focus, and organize ideas and to revise the language, organization, content, and tone of successive drafts in order to fulfill a specific purpose for communicating with a specific audience
- Identify questions and strategies for improving drafts in writing conferences with a teacher
- Given a writing assignment to be completed in a limited amount of time, produce a well developed, well organized, and effective response in correct English and an appropriate voice

TITLE: MEASUREMENT INVOLVING MONEY

GRADE LEVEL/SUBJECT: Grades Kindergarten and up/Math

OVERVIEW: This lesson involves hands-on group activities and workstations to help understand measurement of money.

OBJECTIVES:
1. Identify a penny, nickel, dime, quarter, and a paper dollar
2. In problem solving situations involving money, add and subtract decimals
3. Give values of a penny, nickel, dime, quarter, and dollar
4. Add like and unlike coins
5. Problem solve
6. Estimate
7. Communicate logical arguments clearly to show why a result makes sense

PERFORMANCE STANDARDS:
B.4.2 Determine the number of things in a set by
- combining and arranging (e.g., all possible coin combinations amounting to thirty cents)
- estimation, including rounding

B.4.3 Read, write, and order whole numbers, simple fractions (e.g., halves, fourths, tenths, unit fractions) and commonly-used decimals (monetary units)

B.4.5 In problem-solving situations involving whole numbers, select and efficiently use appropriate computational procedures such as
- recalling the basic facts of addition, subtraction, multiplication, and division
- using mental math (e.g., 37+25, 40x7)
- estimation
- using a calculator

B.4.7 In problem-solving situations involving money, add and subtract decimals

D.4.4 Determine measurements directly by using standard tools to these suggested degrees of accuracy
- monetary value to dollars and cents

RESOURCES AND MATERIALS:

1. School store price information
2. Real or fake money

ACTIVITIES AND PROCEDURE:

1. Divide class up into working groups.
2. Set up different workstations in your classroom. The students can rotate to each work station to meet the individual objectives. As an option to many different work station rotation scenarios, each student in the group can write down their answers for the questions asked at that work station. Then, the students could compare their answers. If there are unlike answers, have the students communicate to each other why they got the answer they did and confirm as a group the correct answer or answers. A calculator may be integrated if desired.

Work Station Ideas:

1. One work station can be an identification center where the students identify by name a penny, nickel, dime, quarter, and dollar. Students can also give values of a penny, nickel, dime, quarter, and dollar.
2. Another work station can be where the students add like coins. For example, a pennies pile, a nickels pile, etc.
3. Another work station could be where the students add unlike coins. Different piles could have different totals to count up to. The students can add exact amounts, round, or estimate.
4. Another work station could be a story problem solving area. For example, some of the questions for this area could include: a. I have some pennies, nickels, and dimes in a money pouch. If I take out four of the coins, how much money do you think I have? b. I have five coins worth $.36, what coins do you think I have? Is there more than one answer? c. Using pennies, nickels, and dimes, how many ways is it possible to make $.36? d. Bob has thirteen pennies. He bought a pencil for five-pennies. How many pennies does Bob have left? e. If Suzie wants to buy a pencil, an eraser, and a folder, how much money will she need? Explain. f. If Bob wants to buy two highlighters, three markers, lead, and a spiral, how much money will he need? Explain. g. About how much should the school store sell a pack of colored pencils for? Explain. h. How many erasable black pens could you buy for $3.00?
5. Another work station could be an estimation station. If some students cannot count exact money, maybe they can estimate the amount of money in a pile. Furthermore, students can make smaller piles of five pennies out of a pile of 25 pennies. What's worth more, five pennies or a nickel?
6. Another work station could be where the students arrange piles of money from least to greatest.
7. Another work station could have about ten different school store items in a pile with a price list next to them. Have the students order the items from least expensive to most expensive or visa versa.

The students can work together or alone to solve and explain their answers. The work stations are flexible depending on class size and capability. You could make several work stations each of identification, value of coins, problem solving, and counting.

LESSON OPTIONS: This authentic hands-on activity is flexible and useful. The students can communicate, compare, verify, and check each other's answers. If some answers don't match, have the students do some problem solving together to find the error. There are many extension activities and discussions that can be integrated, depending on your scope, goals, and age of your students.

TITLE: TIME TO SHOP

GRADE LEVEL/SUBJECT: Grades 2 and up/Math

OVERVIW: This lesson involves hands-on activities and workstations to help understand measurement of money.

OBJECTIVES:

1. In problem solving situations involving money, add and subtract decimals
2. Communicate logical arguments clearly to show why a result makes sense
3. Problem solve

PERFORMANCE STANDARDS:
B.4.7 In problem-solving situations involving money, add and subtract decimals

D.4.4 Determine measurements directly by using standard tools to these suggested degrees of accuracy

- monetary value to dollars and cents

RESOURCES AND MATERIALS:

1. School store price information and items

ACTIVITIES AND PROCEDURE:
Have the students break up into groups of two, three, four, etc. After groups are formed, tell the students that they should pick out five items from the school store. In their groups, have each student total the amount of money it would cost to purchase those five items from the school store and write that total on a piece of paper. Next, have the students subtract that amount from $20.00 to see how much change they would get back. After that, have the students in their groups compare the change received with each member in their group. If they are the same, that's great. If they are not, have the group help each other to figure out where the error was. Return all the items to the school store and choose new items. Do the same process again this time telling students they now have to subtract their total from a different amount other than $20.00.

LESSON OPTIONS

The number of items and the amount of money given to each student is flexible depending on grade level and understanding of addition and subtraction of decimals. Tax and new totals including tax could be introduced. The store could also have a 10% off sale or a ¼ off sale. Find the total of the purchase, subtract 10%, add tax, and get the final amount due. There are many options and concepts that can be incorporated into this activity depending on your scope, goals, and age of your students. As more math and concepts get integrated, like percents and extension questions, more standards can be achieved.

TITLE: MEASUREMENT INVOLVING LENGTH AND WEIGHT

GRADE LEVEL/SUBJECT: Grades 3 and up/Math

OVERVIEW: This lesson involves hands-on group activities and workstations to help understand measurement of length and weight.

OBJECTIVES:

1. Interpret a ruler to the nearest half-inch, quarter-inch, eighth-inch, and centimeter
2. Weigh objects to the nearest ounce, 5 grams, or gram
3. Communicate logical arguments clearly to show why a result makes sense

PERFORMANCE STANDARDS:

D.4.1 Recognize and describe measurable attributes, such as length, liquid capacity, time, weight (mass), temperature, volume, monetary value, and angle size, and identify the appropriate units to measure them

D.4.2 Demonstrate understanding of basic facts, principles, and techniques of measurement, including

- appropriate use of arbitrary and standard units (metric and US Customary)

D.4.3 Read and interpret measuring instruments (e.g., rulers, clocks, thermometers)

D.4.4 Determine measurements directly by using standard tools to these suggested degrees of accuracy

- length to the nearest half-inch or nearest cm
- weight (mass) to the nearest ounce or nearest 5 grams

RESOURCES AND MATERIALS:

1. School store and store items
2. Measuring devices to measure an objects length to a specified amount and measure an objects weight to a specified amount.

ACTIVITIES AND PROCEDURE:

1. Divide the class into working groups.
2. Set up different workstations in your room. The students can rotate to each station to meet the individual objectives and performance standards.
3. The first few work stations can be a measurement of length station. Students can measure chosen objects from the school store to the nearest specified degree of accuracy.
4. The second few work stations can be a measurement of weight station. Students can weigh chosen objects from the school store to the specified degree of accuracy.
5. Have the students in their groups compare their findings with each member in their group. If they are the same, that's great. If they are not, have the group help each other to figure out where the error was. Have the students compare and contrast their answers and work together to come up with the correct amount.

LESSON OPTIONS

The numbers of workstations are flexible depending on class size, grade, and capabilities. Different workstations can be set up to measure different degrees of accuracy. For example, there could be four different stations, one each to measure to the nearest inch, half-inch, quarter-inch, and eighth-inch. The same procedure can be used for different degrees of weight. Have a couple of each of the degrees of accuracy stations. Students get a better understanding of how long something is when actual objects are measured instead of lines on a piece of paper. Measure the length, width, and height of the school store to the nearest degree of accuracy. Have the students communicate, verify, and compare the results with each other. If there is a disagreement, do some problem-solving to find the true solution or solutions. Ask questions like: Why is this item so small but weigh so much? Does the length of an item necessarily mean it is going to weigh more or less? Etc.

TITLE: NUMBER OPERATIONS AND RELATIONS INVOLVING MONEY

GRADE LEVEL/SUBJECT: Grades 3 and up/Math

OVERVIEW: This lesson involves hands-on group activities and workstations to help understand some number operations and relations through the use of the school store.

OBJECTIVES:
1. Rounding to the nearest dollar and tenths (dimes place)
2. Write monetary units as decimals
3. Use estimation when solving word problems
4. Add and subtract decimals in problem-solving situations involving money
5. Order monetary units
6. Make change
7. Communicate logical arguments clearly to show why a result makes sense

PERFORMANCE STANDARDS:

B.4.1 Represent and explain whole numbers, decimals, and fractions with
- physical materials
- verbal descriptions

B.4.2 Determine the number of things in a set by
- grouping and counting (e.g., by threes, fives, hundreds)
- combining and arranging (e.g., all possible coin combinations amounting to thirty cents)
- estimation, including rounding

B.4.5 In problem-solving situations involving whole numbers, select and efficiently use appropriate computational procedures such as
- recalling the basic facts of addition, subtraction, multiplication, and division
- using mental math (e.g., 37+25, 40x7)
- estimation
- selecting and applying algorithms for addition, subtraction, multiplication, and division
- using a calculator

B.4.7 In problem-solving situations involving money, add and subtract decimals

D.4.4 Determine measurements directly by using standard tools to these suggested degrees of accuracy
- monetary value to dollars and cents

RESOURCES AND MATERIALS:
School store items and price list

ACTIVITIES AND PROCEDURE:

1. Divide the class up into working groups. The students can work together or alone to solve and explain their answers.

2. Set up different workstations in your classroom. The students can rotate to each station to meet the individual objectives.

Work Station Ideas:

1. One station can have piles of money (fake or real) for the students to count. After they have counted the money and written the appropriate sums on their paper, have them round each sum to the nearest dollar and/or dime. Have the students compare and discuss answers.

2. Another station can have word problems, along with a price list, on separate sheets of paper for the students to solve. These questions could include: a. If Suzie wants to buy a pencil, an eraser, and a folder, about how much money will she need? Explain. b. If Bob wants to buy two highlighters, three markers, lead, and a spiral, about how much money will he need? Explain. c. About how much should the school store sell a pack of colored pencils for? Explain. d. About how many erasable black pens could you buy for $2.00? e. I have some pennies, nickels, and dimes in a money pouch. If I take out five of the coins, how much money do you think I have? f. I have five coins worth $.40; what coins do you think I have? Is there more than one answer? g. Using pennies, nickels, and dimes, how many ways is it possible to make $.56?

3. Another workstation could be some role-playing of clerks and buyers. The clerks are the sales people behind the store taking the orders and adding up the total of the purchases. The buyers are the people buying the school store items with the money they were given at the beginning of class. The buyers also need to be adding up or estimating the total of their purchase to make sure they have enough money and to make sure the clerk didn't add the total of the sale incorrectly. Both the clerk and the buyer need to make sure the correct amount of change is given.

4. Another workstation could have about six different school store items in a pile with a price list next to them. Have the students order the items from least expensive to most expensive or visa versa

LESSON OPTIONS

This authentic hands-on learning activity can be a useful tool in the classroom. The types of learning stations, number of students per group, activities at each station, and rotation through the stations are flexible depending on the class's size, age of your students, your scope, and your goals.

When the students are in their groups, have them communicate, work together, compare, and verify each other's answers. If a mistake is found, have the students do some problem solving, within their group, to correct and understand their group's mistakes.

TITLE: INTERPRETING DATA

GRADE LEVEL/SUBJECT: Grades 4 and up/Math

OVERVIEW: An activity that provides development of data interpretation and communication

OBJECTIVES:

1) Use reasoning abilities to:
    a) Evaluate information
    b) Identify relationships
    c) Formulate questions for further exploration
    d) Justify statements

2) Develop effective oral and written presentations that include:
    a) Appropriate use of technology
    b) The conventions of mathematical discourse
    c) Mathematical language
    d) Clear organization of ideas and procedures
    e) Understanding of purpose and audience

PERFORMANCE STANDARDS:

A.4.1 Use reasoning abilities to

- perceive patterns
- identify relationships
- formulate questions for further exploration

A.4.2 Communicate mathematical ideas in a variety of ways, including words, numbers, symbols, pictures, charts, graphs, tables, diagrams, and models

B.4.7 In problem-solving situations involving money, add and subtract decimals

E.4.3 In problem-solving situations, read, extract, and use information presented in graphs, tables, or charts

A.4.5 Use media and technology to create and present information

- use draw, paint or graphics

A.8.5 Use media and technology to create and present information

- use draw, paint, or graphics software to create visuals that will enhance a class project or report

RESOURCES AND MATERIALS:
School store data. You can use your current data you have collected from operating your school store business. The data in Figure 5-3 and 5-4 was previously gathered and does not correlate to the data in the "Sample Sales, Profits, and Inventory Spreadsheet" spreadsheet in Appendix A.

Computer (optional, but needed if you are trying to incorporate media and technology instead of graphing by hand)

ACTIVITIES AND PROCEDURE:

1. Have the students tabulate the sales and profits from items in the school store.
2. Have the students make bar graphs of the sales and profits either with a computer or by hand (similar Figures 5-3 and 5-4).
3. Have each student do a profit and sales analogy on different school store items using these extension questions:

A. Describe the two graphs. What does each graph tell you?
B. What school store item had the most and least amount of sales? Why do you think so?
C. What school store item had the most and least amount of profit? Why do you think so?
D. What are some things that might happen if we raised the prices of certain items in the school store?
E. What are some things that might happen if we lowered the prices of certain items in the school store?
F. Why do you think that the item that sold the most didn't make the most amount of profit?
G. How would you price an item at the school store and why?
H. What are some things that determine the amount of sales?
I. What are some things that determine the amount of profit?
J. Create a short essay persuading someone why some school store items should be sold or not be sold.

Figure 5-3

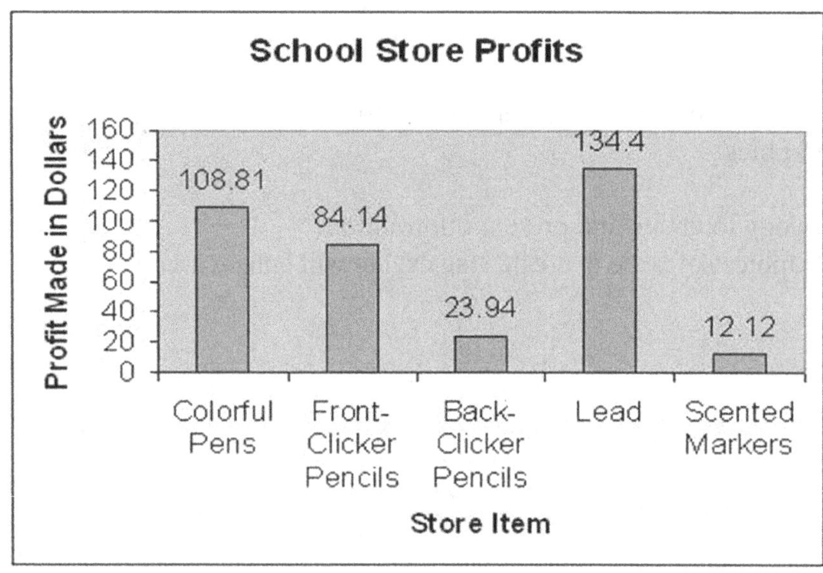

Figure 5-4

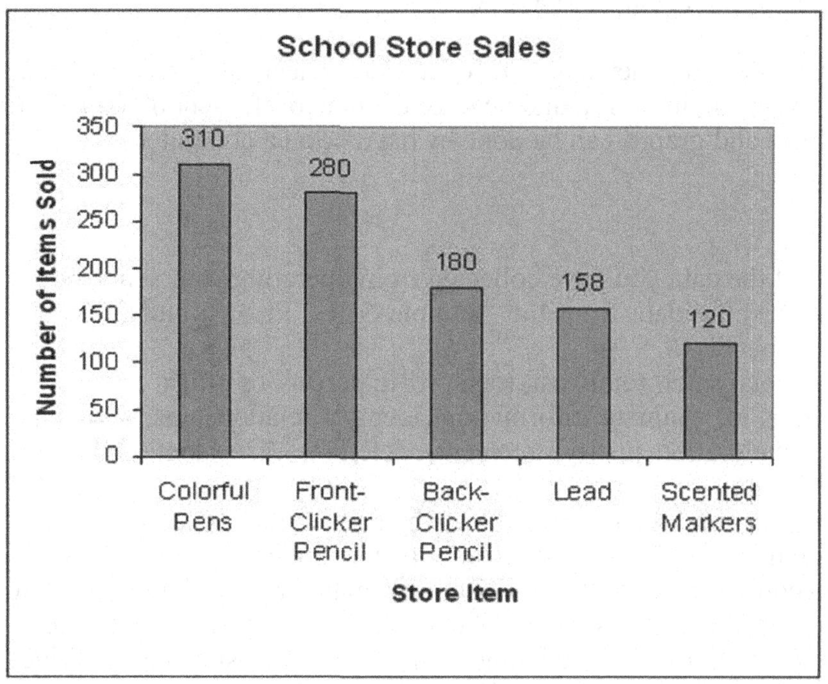

LESSON OPTIONS:

This hands-on activity is a good example of the types of business practices that go on everyday to help analyze sales and profit. Students can become involved in their own financial upkeep of the school store business. This activity can be modified depending on your scope, goals, and age of your students.

A good spiral extension activity is that the students could write an informational or persuasive speech or essay about a topic, an issue, an idea, a comment, or findings regarding the school store or the activity they just accomplished. This activity can also be integrated into computer classes or computers can be used to present some of the findings regarding the school store data.

TITLE: SPREADSHEET AND GRAPHING ACTIVITY

GRADE LEVEL/SUBJECT: Grades 5 and up/Math/Technology Education

OVERVIEW: An activity that provides development of a spreadsheet and graphs of that spreadsheet so students can evaluate, interpret, and analyze the data of the school store. The development of the spreadsheet and graphs can be done by hand or on a computer.

OBJECTIVES:

1. Make a spreadsheet of the data you have collected from operating your school store business or you can use the data from the "Sample Sales, Profits, and Inventory Spreadsheet" from Appendix A.
2. Determine total sold, total sales, total cost, total profit, percent of profit
3. Use reasoning abilities to: evaluate information, identify relationships, formulate questions for further exploration, justify statements, defend work, evaluate strategies, interpret and analyze data
4. Communicate logical arguments clearly to show why a result makes sense
5. Develop effective oral and written presentations that include: appropriate use of technology, the conventions of mathematical discourse, mathematical language, clear organization of ideas and procedures, and understanding the purpose of audience
6. Analyze non-routine problems by modeling, illustrating, guessing, simplifying, generalizing, and shifting to another point of view
7. Calculate percent of sales
8. Round to the nearest tenth
9. Change decimals to percents
10. Make pie graphs/bar graphs
11. Add and subtract multiply and divide decimals
12. Calculate unit cost
13. Turn decimals to percents and percents to decimals

PERFORMANCE STANDARDS:
E.4.1 Work with data in the context of real-world situations by

- formulating questions that lead to data collection and analysis
- determining what data to collect and when and how to collect them
- collecting, organizing, and displaying data
- drawing reasonable conclusions based on data

E.4.3 In problem-solving situations, read, extract, and use information presented in graphs, tables, or charts
B.4.7 In problem-solving situations involving money, add and subtract decimals
B.8.1 Read, represent, and interpret various rational numbers (whole numbers, integers, decimals, fractions, and percents) with verbal descriptions, geometric models, and mathematical notation (e.g., expanded, scientific, exponential)
B.8.5 Apply proportional thinking in a variety of problem situations that include, but are not limited to

- percents, including those greater than 100 and less than one (e.g., discounts, rate of increase or decrease, sales tax)

B.8.7 In problem-solving situations, select and use appropriate computational procedures with rational numbers such as

- calculating mentally
- estimating
- using technology (e.g., scientific calculators, spreadsheets)

RESOURCES AND MATERIALS
Price sheet of store items
Unit cost of each item
Tallied data stating the number of each item sold from the school store (optional).
Spreadsheet and graphing material
Software that provides spreadsheet and graphing capabilities (this process can also be done by hand like in this activity).

ACTIVITIES AND PROCEDURE:

1. Make a spreadsheet of the data you have collected from operating your school store business similar to the "Sample Sales, Profits, and Inventory Spreadsheet" in Appendix A, or use the data from the "Sample Sales, Profits, and Inventory Spreadsheet" in Appendix A. You can make a spreadsheet of everything or a few things, depending on your scope and goals. The data can be accumulated after sales from one day, one week, one month, or several months.
2. After the number of each school store item sold has been tallied, enter the total sold number in the (**total sold**) column of the spreadsheet.
3. In the next column (**selling price**), enter the selling price of each item in the school store being tabulated.
4. In the next column (**total sales),** calculate the amount for each item by multiplying the total sold number by the selling price.
5. In the next column (**cost price),** enter the cost price for each item. The cost price is the unit cost for that item. For example, if you paid $1.00 plus a 5% sales tax for two pens, the cost price would be $1.05 divided by 2 = $.53 each.
6. In the next column (**total cost),** calculate the total cost by multiplying the total sold number by the cost price amount.
7. In the next column (**total profit),** calculate the total profit by subtracting the total cost amount from the total sales amount.
8. In the next column, the (**sub-total)** amount for each category is determined by adding together the profit for each item in that category. For example, from the "Sample Sales, Profits, and Inventory Spreadsheet" in Appendix A, the sub-total for the Markers is $19.36. That amount was calculated by adding together all the different types of markers in that category (highlighters-$7.70 + smelly markers-$11.66).
9. Next, add together all the sub-total amounts in each category to get the grand total profit.
10. In the column next to the sub-total, the (percent of sales) amounts are determined by dividing the sub-total amount of each category by the grand total profit. For example, from the "Sample Sales, Profits, and Inventory Spreadsheet" in Appendix A, the sub-total profit for markers is $19.36. Therefore, $19.36 divided by $251.97 = .07683 or about 7.7%. Do this process for each category you want to graph.
11. Bar graphs can be made of any data that you desire so the students can get a visual interpretation of that data. Bar graphs can be made by putting the store item on the bottom (x-axis) and the total sold, total sales, total profit, or percent of sales along the side (y-axis), depending on what you and your students feel like graphing (see figures 5-3 and 5-4 in the "Interpreting Data" activity in appendix G).

12. Pie graphs can be a bit more involved, depending on your scope and goals. The following procedure describes how to make a pie graph, by hand, of "percent of sales" so students can get a better visual of the data. You don't have to do a percent of sales pie graph. You can make a pie graph of many types of data. The data for this pie graph comes from the "percent of sales" data in the "Sample Sales, Profits, and Inventory Spreadsheet" located in appendix A.

First, on an 8.5" x 11" sheet of paper or larger, draw a circle about the size of a coffee can. A large circle is easier to use.

Next, draw a radius in the circle. This will be used as your base line when measuring degrees.

The first percent of sales category is going to be lead. Lead was 9.7% of total sales. So, 9.7% of 360 degrees = .097 x 360 = about 35 degrees. So, from your base line (radius), measure up 35 degrees with a protractor. Make a mark at 35 degrees and draw a line from the center of the circle to that mark. That section of the pie is now your percent of sales for lead.

The next category (piece of the pie) can be markers. Markers were 7.7% of total sales. So, 7.7% of 360 degrees = .077 x 360 = about 28 degrees. Then, from the line you drew for lead, measure up 28 degrees from that line and make another line. This section of the pie is your percent of sales for markers. Follow this procedure for paper (11.7%), pencils (19.2%), pens (22.6%), and candy (24.3%). The 24.3% for candy comes from combining the chips percent with the candy bars and gum percents. Plus, I combined the percent of sales for erasers, foam grips, and folders, because their percent of sales was so small. Therefore, 1.5% + 1.8% + 1.4% = 4.7%. So, 4.7% of 360 degrees = .047 x 360 = about 17 degrees.

After the pie graph activity you may want to ask a few extension questions such as:

1. What school store item had the most and least amount of profits, sales, and percent of sales, etc. and why do you think so?

2. What are some things that might happen if we lowered or raised the price of some of the items sold? Do you think profit would go up or down, and why? Would we sell more or less if the price went up or down and why?

3. Why do you think that the items that sold the most did not make the most amount of profit?

4. How would you price an item at the school store and why?

5. What are some things that determine the amount of sales, profit, and percent of sales and why do you think so?

LESSON OPTIONS:

This real-world activity is a good example of the types of business practices that go on everyday to determine sales and profit. Students can become involved in their own financial upkeep of the school store business. These activities can be modified depending on your scope, goals, and age of your students. A good spiral extension activity is that the students could write an informational or persuasive speech or essay about a topic, an issue, an idea, a comment, or findings regarding the school store or the activity they just accomplished. These activities can also be integrated into computer classes or computers can be used to present some of the findings regarding the school store data.

TITLE: ANALYZING COST, PROFIT, AND REVENUE OF A SCHOOL STORE

GRADE LEVEL/SUBJECT: Grades 6 and up/Math

OVERVIEW: An activity that provides development of tables, graphs, and equations while analyzing cost, revenue, and profit of the school store.

OBJECTIVES:

1. Work with linear patterns in a variety of ways
2. Describe a real-world phenomenon that a given graph might represent
3. Analyze cost, profit, and revenue of an item at the school store
4. Graph linear equations
5. Write and evaluate linear equations
6. Communicate logical arguments clearly to show why a result makes sense

PERFORMANCE STANDARDS:

E.8.1 Work with data in the context of real-world situations by:

- formulating questions that lead to data collection and analysis

E.8.2 Organize and display data from statistical investigations using:

- appropriate tables, graphs, and/or charts (e.g., circle, bar or line for multiple sets of data)

E.8.4 Use the results of data analysis to:

- make predictions
- develop convincing arguments
- draw conclusions

E.8.5 Compare several sets of data to generate, test, and, as the data dictate, confirm or deny hypotheses

F.8.2 Work with linear and nonlinear patterns and relationships in a variety of ways, including

- representing them with tables, with graphs, and with algebraic expressions, equations, and inequalities
- describing and interpreting their graphical representations (e.g., slope, rate of change, intercepts)
- using them as models of real-world phenomena
- describing a real-world phenomenon that a given graph might represent

F.8.4 Use linear equations and inequalities in a variety of ways, including

- writing them to represent problem situations and to express generalizations
- solving them by different methods (e.g., informally, graphically, with formal properties, with technology)

RESOURCES AND MATERIALS:

School store information regarding the number of items sold, unit cost, and selling price
Graph paper

ACTIVITIES AND PROCEDURE:

During the school year, you decide to analyze the cost, revenue, and profit of the hottest selling pen in the school store (see gel pen in the "Sample Sales, Profits, and Inventory Spreadsheet" located in appendix A). So, after selling all 14 of the popular pens, you analyze the cost, profit, and revenue of the hottest selling pen by making tables and linear graphs. You remember from stocking the school store that a pack of fourteen pens cost \$9.99 plus a 5% sales tax (\$.50). So, the total cost for fourteen pens is \$9.99 + tax or \$10.49. Therefore, the unit cost for these hot pens, to the nearest penny, is \$.75 (\$10.49 divided by 14). You have been selling the pens for \$1.10 each (revenue).

1. (a) Make a table of values for the cost, revenue, and profit of the gel pen. To do this, set up a table of values in which one column corresponds to the number of pens sold and a second column corresponds to the total cost, revenue, and profit to the business when that number of pens has been sold. For example, the beginning of the cost table has been started below. \$10.50 was used instead of \$10.49 for easier calculations and graphing.

COST TABLE

Sold (x)	Total Cost (y)
0	\$10.50
1	\$9.75
2	
3	
4	
5	
6	
7	
8	
9	
10	
11	
12	
13	
14	

When *x*, the total number of pens sold increases by one, how does *y*, the total cost to the business decrease?

(b). Create a revenue table.

REVENUE TABLE

Sold (x)	Total Revenue (y)
0	
1	
2	
3	
4	
5	
6	
7	
8	
9	
10	
11	
12	
13	
14	

When x, the total number of pens sold increases by one, how does y, the total revenue to the business increase?

(c). Create a profit table. Profit is found by subtracting cost from revenue. Find the appropriate difference, and create a table that shows profit in relation to the number of pens sold.

PROFIT TABLE

Sold (x)	Total Revenue (y)
0	
1	
2	
3	
4	
5	
6	
7	
8	
9	
10	
11	
12	
13	
14	

When x, the total number of pens sold, increases by one, how does y, the total profit to the business, increase?

(d) Find the linear cost equation. Hint: y = mx + b____________________________________
(e) Find the linear revenue equation. Hint: y = ( )x ___________________________________
(f) Find the linear profit equation. ____
(g). Graph the three equations on one graph (coordinate plane). Label your axis.

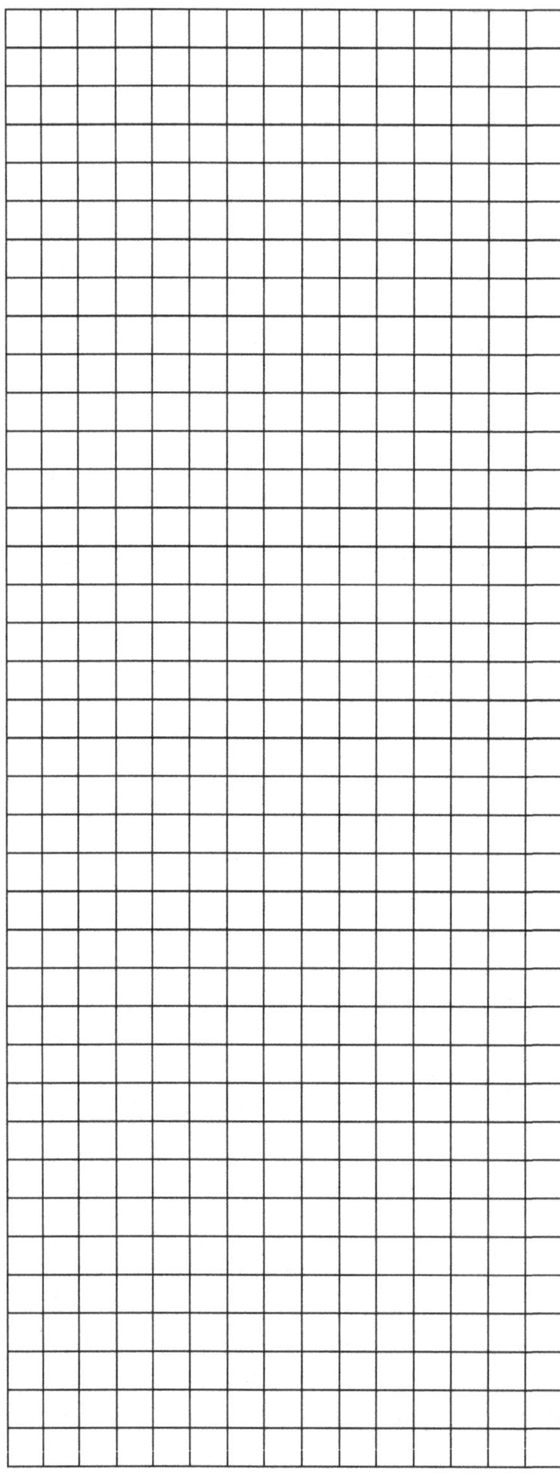

2. How many pens would you have to sell to break even? ______________________

3. How many pens do you think you could actually sell in one week or one month? What would be your weekly or monthly revenue?

4. If you wanted to make fifteen dollars profit, how many pens would you have to sell?

5. Do you think it is a good idea to sell this pen at that price? What do you think will happen to the graphs of cost, revenue, and profit if you raised or lowered the price of the pens?

LESSON OPTIONS:

This real-world activity is a good example of the types of business practices that go on everyday to determine sales, revenue, and profit. Students can become involved in their own financial upkeep of the school store business. These activities can be modified depending on your scope, goals, and age of your students. A good spiral extension activity is that the students could write an informational essay about an idea, a comment, or findings regarding the school store or the activity they just accomplished. These activities can also be integrated into computer classes or computers can be used to present some of the findings regarding the school store data.

BRAINTEASERS

The following school store brainteasers may be used at various grade levels and can be modified to meet your scope and goals.

Mathematics as problem solving

Combination Situations

1. Find the number of school store purchase outcomes that can be determined with $.45 and $1.75.

2. I have some pennies, nickels, and dimes in my pocket. I put three of the coins in my hand. How much money do you think I have in my hand?

3. I have six coins worth $.42. What coins do you think I have? Is there more than one answer?

4. Maria had some pencils in her desk. She put 5 more in her desk. Then she had 14. How many pencils did she have in her desk to start with?

Mathematics as communication

1. Students can write a letter to tell a friend about something they have learned involving math or the school store.

2. Have students keep journals.

3. Have the students write the procedure for adding/subtracting/multiplying/dividing fractions and/or decimals. Then have the students exchange papers and see if the person they exchanged with can follow the procedure and achieve the correct answer from the procedure they followed.

Mathematics as reasoning

1. Make a number line from $0.00 to $5.00, or whatever spread and increments you feel is reasonable. Have a student pick out a school store item. Have the other students guess what the item is by where the student who picked the item places that item on the number line.

2. Rethinking the role of computation. Three schoolteachers want to buy all the fourth grade students in a class a school store item. Mr. Smith spent $26.94. Since the three teachers wanted to share the cost of the purchase, Mr. Smith used his calculator to determine that each teacher should pay him $13.47. Is this answer reasonable? Explain.

Mathematical connections

1. What is the most expensive school store item? How much is it? What is the least expensive school store item? How much is it? Write a sentence comparing the two items.

Estimation

1. Estimate how much a total bill may be at the school store when five pens are purchased.

2. Now, estimate that bill including tax.

Number sense and numeration

1. Here are 144 pencils. How many piles of 10 could you make?

Statistics and Probability

1. We need to know whether we have more students using pens or pencils in our school. What can we do to decide?

2. Which display would we use to find out what school store items students like most?

ESSAY 1

What does it take to be a good employee? In your essay, describe the characteristics of a good employee. Give specific details to support your views. Use your personal observations, experiences, and knowledge to support your essay.

In preparation for your essay, you should take the following steps:

- Read the directions and the topic carefully
- Plan your essay before you write.
- Before you turn in your essay, reread what you have written and make any changes that will improve your essay. Your essay should be long enough to develop your topic adequately.

ESSAY 2

Today our workplaces and neighborhoods are composed of people with diverse backgrounds. For this reason, it is important for people to find ways to get along with each other. Write an essay explaining how people with diverse backgrounds can get along together. Give specific details to support your views. Use your personal observations, experiences, and knowledge to support your essay.

In preparation for your essay, you should take the following steps:

- Read the directions and the topic carefully
- Plan your essay before you write.
- Before you turn in your essay, reread what you have written and make any changes that will improve your essay. Your essay should be long enough to develop your topic adequately.

ESSAY 3

Why do so many customers complain about poor service in stores and restaurants? Give specific details to support your views. Use your personal observations, experiences, and knowledge to support your essay.

In preparation for your essay, you should take the following steps:

- Read the directions and the topic carefully
- Plan your essay before you write.
- Before you turn in your essay, reread what you have written and make any changes that will improve your essay. Your essay should be long enough to develop your topic adequately.

ESSAY 4

Who is more courageous—a person who asks for help when he or she needs it or a person who works things out alone?

Give specific details to support your views. Use your personal observations, experiences, and knowledge to support your essay.

In preparation for your essay, you should take the following steps:

- Read the directions and the topic carefully
- Plan your essay before you write.
- Before you turn in your essay, reread what you have written and make any changes that will improve your essay. Your essay should be long enough to develop your topic adequately.

ESSAY 5

How important is it to set goals in life? Explain your answer.

Give specific details to support your views. Use your personal observations, experiences, and knowledge to support your essay.

In preparation for your essay, you should take the following steps:

- Read the directions and the topic carefully
- Plan your essay before you write.
- Before you turn in your essay, reread what you have written and make any changes that will improve your essay. Your essay should be long enough to develop your topic adequately.

ESSAY 6

If there were more hours in a day, do you think people would spend them working or relaxing?

Give specific details to support your views. Use your personal observations, experiences, and knowledge to support your essay.

In preparation for your essay, you should take the following steps:

- Read the directions and the topic carefully
- Plan your essay before you write.
- Before you turn in your essay, reread what you have written and make any changes that will improve your essay. Your essay should be long enough to develop your topic adequately.

ESSAY 7

Everyone feels angry at one time or another. What do you think is the best way to deal with anger?

Give specific details to support your views. Use your personal observations, experiences, and knowledge to support your essay.

In preparation for your essay, you should take the following steps:

- Read the directions and the topic carefully
- Plan your essay before you write.
- Before you turn in your essay, reread what you have written and make any changes that will improve your essay. Your essay should be long enough to develop your topic adequately.

ESSAY 8

If you could give one piece of advice about life, what would it be?

Give specific details to support your views. Use your personal observations, experiences, and knowledge to support your essay.

In preparation for your essay, you should take the following steps:

- Read the directions and the topic carefully
- Plan your essay before you write.
- Before you turn in your essay, reread what you have written and make any changes that will improve your essay. Your essay should be long enough to develop your topic adequately.

ESSAY 9

Describe the events leading up to the opening of the school store.

Give specific details to support your views. Use your personal observations, experiences, and knowledge to support your essay.

In preparation for your essay, you should take the following steps:

- Read the directions and the topic carefully
- Plan your essay before you write.
- Before you turn in your essay, reread what you have written and make any changes that will improve your essay. Your essay should be long enough to develop your topic adequately.

ESSAY 10

Write a letter to persuade someone to shop at the school store. Include the features and benefits of the store.

Give specific details to support your views. Use your personal observations, experiences, and knowledge to support your essay.

In preparation for your essay, you should take the following steps:

- Read the directions and the topic carefully
- Plan your essay before you write.
- Before you turn in your essay, reread what you have written and make any changes that will improve your essay. Your essay should be long enough to develop your topic adequately.

SECTION 6

ASSEMBLY PLANS FOR THE BIGGEST, MOST DURABLE MOBILE SCHOOL STORE

There are many reasons why a school may want to develop and operate a school store, or better, **a mobile school store.** Maybe the school wants a **continuous fundraiser** with access to a **variety of locations** and customers, with **easy self-locking storage**. Maybe the school is interested in providing youth with interesting and exciting work experiences that **promote lifelong learning**, and maximize academic success by connecting school to work. Whatever the reason, a mobile school store has **many features and benefits.**

The mobile store can be assembled by many different people. One such group of people is the junior high or high school shop class. Other people that could assemble the school store are the school's maintenance staff, fellow woodworking volunteers, or general handymen in your community.

MOBILE SCHOOL STORE FEATURES

Solid Construction
Self-locking
Easy Mobility
12 Adjustable Shelves
Dimensions 48"L x 18"W x 42"H
48" x 36 ¾" Acrylic Front

MOBILE SCHOOL STORE BENEFITS

Continuous Fundraiser
Display Merchandise Effectively
Sell in Different Locations
Easy Storage with Secure Locking

MATERIALS NEEDED

Some of the following materials can be changed to meet your needs. For example:

- **The size of the castors, hasps, and handles do not have to be exactly like the materials list.**
- **You may want to adjust the number of screws used.**
- **Instead of painting the store, you may want to stain and polyurethane the wood instead, or leave the wood natural looking.**
- **The acrylic/plastic sheet used on the front of the store and shelves does not have to be ¼ inch. ¼ inch is recommended for shelf strength. You may not need shelves that strong because of what you are going to sell.**
- **The lumber does not have to be birch. The wood can be oak, or whatever you think you may need, depending on the durability you want.**
- **The lumber does not have to be veneer plywood. You can use regular plywood if you choose. Veneer plywood makes the surfaces of the store smooth.**

The prices that are listed are estimates. The actual cost of the materials will depend on the store where you purchase them and the sales tax you pay in your state.

HARDWARE

QTY	DESCRIPTION	PRICE EACH	TOTAL
2	48 INCH CONTINUOUS HINGES	$10.00	$20.00
2	3 INCH FIXED CASTORS	$7.00	$14.00
2	3 INCH SWIVEL CASTORS	$7.00	$14.00
4	3 ½" HASPS	$3.00	$12.00
2	5 ¾" HANDLES	$3.00	$6.00
24	1 ¼" PAN HEAD SCREW	$.04	$1.00
24	2" DRYWALL/MULTI PURPOSE SCREW	$.04	$1.00
12	36" ADJUSTABLE SHELF BRACKETS/ SUPPORT STRIPS	$1.50	$18.00
4	BAGS OF SUPPORT/SHELF CLIPS AND NAILS (12/BAG = 48) FOR SHELF BRACKETS	$3.00	$12.00
16	¼" HEX NUTS OR LOCK NUTS	$.04	$1.00
16	¼" X 1 ¼" CARRIAGE BOLT/HEX CAP BOLT	$.04	$1.00
16	¼" LOCK WASHERS	$.04	$1.00
1	OZ. BOTTLE CARPENTERS WOOD GLUE	$1.00	$1.00
1	PAINT or STAIN AND POLYURATHANE	$15.00	$15.00

LUMBER

QTY.	DESCRIPTION	PRICE EACH	TOTAL
1	¾" X 4' X 8' BIRCH VENEER PLYWOOD	$40.00	$40.00
1	¾" X 4' X 4' BIRCH VENEER PLYWOOD	$20.00	$20.00

ACRYLIC

QTY.	DESCRIPTION	PRICE EACH	TOTAL
1	¼" X 4' X 8' PLASTIC SHEET/ACRILIC/ PLEXIGLASS	$120.00	$120.00

TOTAL = $297.00
+ 17. 82 **6%Tax**
$314.82

TOOLS

A. Table saw or skill saw (table saw may be better for straighter cuts)
B. Marking Device
C. Measuring Device
D. Straight Edge
E. Drill and 1/8" and/or 1/16" drill bit for pilot holes
F. Electric drill and/or a battery powered drill
G. Screwdriver
H. Hammer

ASSEMBLY INSTRUCTIONS

STEP 1. CUTTING THE ENDS, PARTITIONS, TOP, BOTTOM, BACK 1, AND BACK 2

Note: The pieces that are going to be cut and assembled are *italicized.* The pieces of wood to be cut in figures 6-1 and 6-2 are not proportional to the whole sheet of plywood. This was done to make the diagram easier to read.

When cutting the plywood, it is best to use a small-toothed saw blade. The plywood can be cut with a skill saw but a table saw will result in straighter cuts. Remember that the saw blade is about 1/8-inch thick and has to be taken into consideration when cutting so that the pieces don't end up too short, or not the same size. Also remember to cut slowly as to not splinter the plywood.

1a. From the ¾" X 4' X 8' sheet of plywood, cut the *top, bottom,* 2 *ends,* and the 2 *partitions*. You may want to cut the pieces going with the grain of the wood because it will look better when built. The grain runs the length of the sheet of plywood. There are portions of the plywood sheet that won't be used. These portions are labeled as leftover. The length and width of the *top*, *bottom*, 2 *ends*, and 2 *partitions* are given in figure 6-1 below.

Figure 6-1

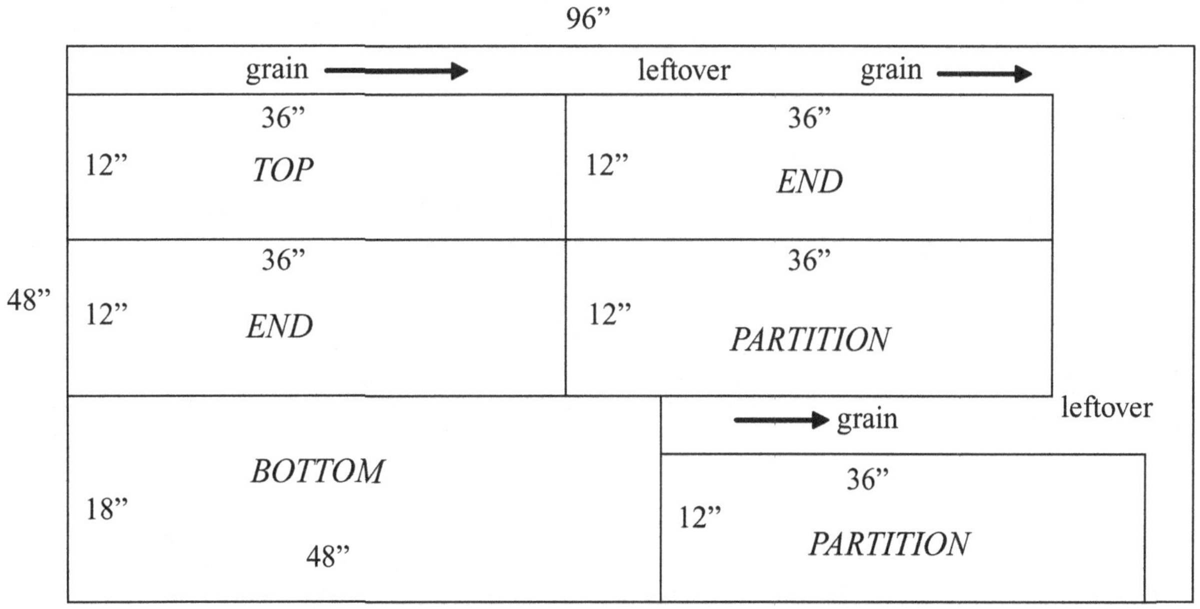

96"
grain →
leftover
grain →
36"
12"
TOP
36"
12"
END
48"
36"
12"
END
36"
12"
PARTITION
→ grain
leftover
BOTTOM
18"
48"
36"
12"
PARTITION

1b. From the ¾" X 4' X 4' sheet of plywood, cut the 2 *backs* of the store. You may want to cut the *backs* going with the grain of the wood, like shown in the diagram below. There are portions of the plywood sheet that won't be used. These portions are labeled as leftover. The length and width of *back 1* and *back 2* are given in figure 6-2 below.

Figure 6-2

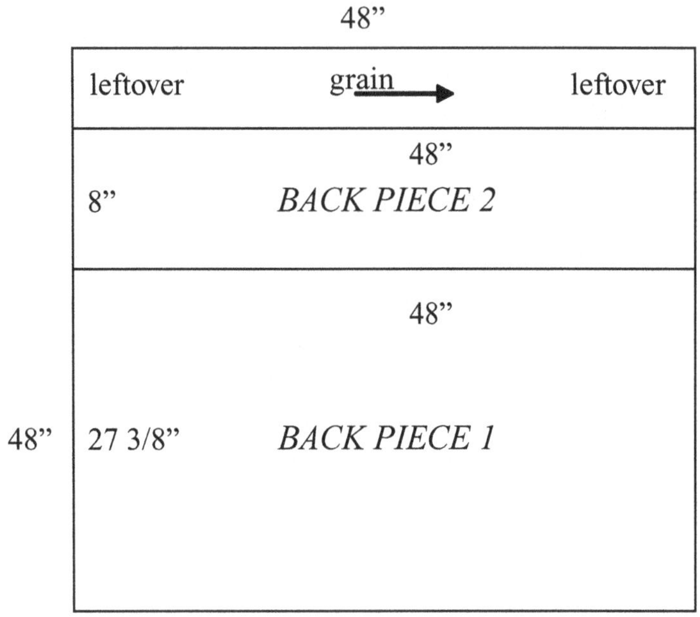

48"

leftover grain → leftover

48"

8" *BACK PIECE 2*

48"

48" 27 3/8" *BACK PIECE 1*

STEP 2. PREPARING TO ASSEMBLE THE ENDS AND PARTITIONS TO THE TOP AND BOTTOM

2a. Trace with a marking device around the parts of the *ends* and *partitions* that are positioned on the *bottom*, so as to draw an outline of exactly where the *ends* and *partitions* are going to be fastened to the *bottom*. To do this, set the *bottom* on the floor. Place the *ends* and *partitions* perpendicular (90 degree angle) on their ends and trace. Re-measure and re-check to be sure that the outlines are where they need to be. Also, remember that there needs to be the same amount of space between the *ends* and *partitions* (15 inches) and there needs to be the same amount of space between the edges of the *partitions* and *ends*, and the edges of the *bottom* (3 inches). See figures 6-3 and 6-4 below.

2b. After tracing, drill pilot holes through the *bottom* where the *ends* and *partitions* will be fastened to the *bottom*. A 1/16-inch or a 1/8-inch drill bit can be used for the pilot holes. When centering the 3 pilot holes in the outline of the *partitions* and *ends*, stay about 1 ½-2" from the end of the outline of the *partitions* and *ends* for the outer two pilot holes and then drill the third pilot hole in the middle of the other two pilot holes. See figures 6-3 and 6-4 below.

Figure 6-3

TOP VIEW

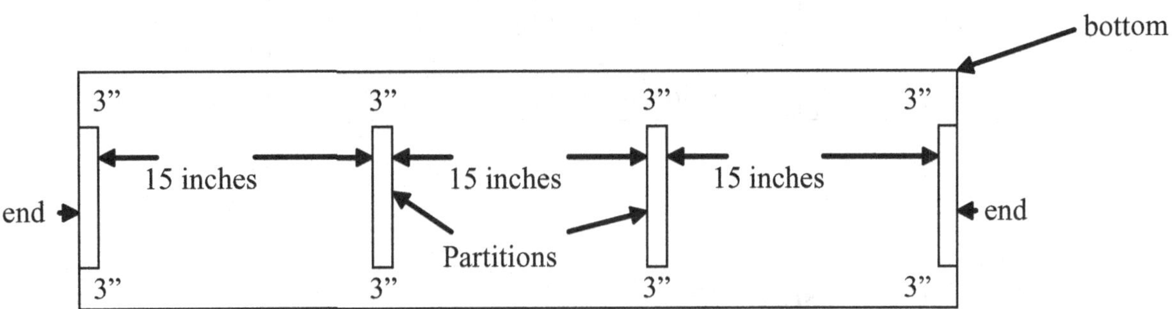

Figure 6-4

SIDE VIEW

end
partitions
end
bottom

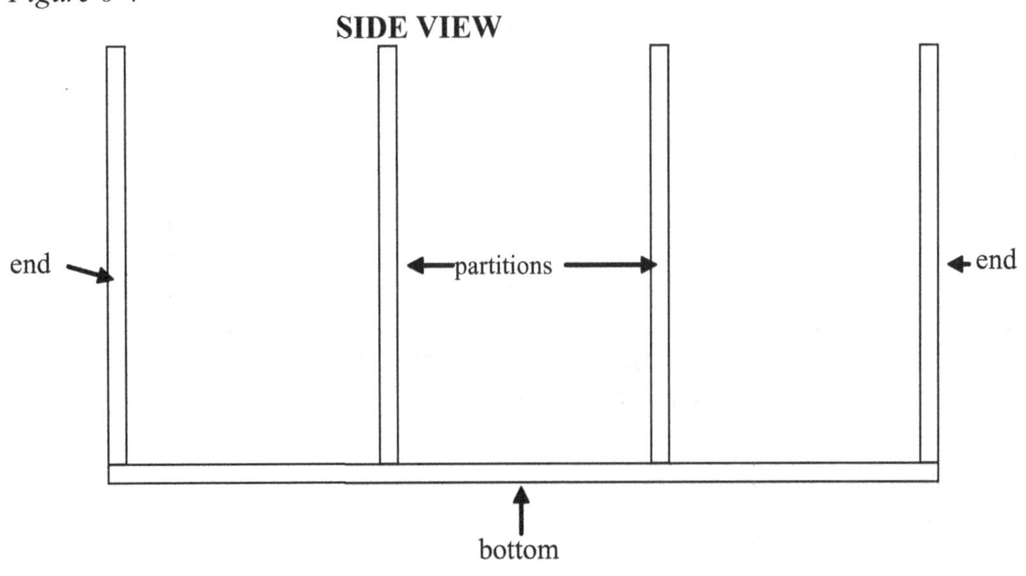

2c. Trace with a marking device around the parts of the *ends* and *partitions* that are positioned on the *top*, so as to draw an outline of exactly where the *ends* and *partitions* are going to be fastened to the *top*. To do this, set the *top* on the floor. Place the *ends* and *partitions* perpendicular (90 degree angle) on their ends and trace. Re-measure and re-check to be sure that the outlines are where they need to be. Also, remember that there needs to be the same amount of space between the *ends* and *partitions* (15 inches). See figures 6-5 and 6-6.

2d . After tracing, drill pilot holes through the *top* where the *ends* and *partitions* will be fastened to the *top*. A 1/8-inch or 1/16-inch drill bit should be used for the pilot holes. When centering the 3 pilot holes in the outline of the *partitions* and *ends*, stay about 1 ½-2" from the end of the outline of the *partitions* and *ends* for the outer two pilot holes and then drill the third pilot hole in the middle of the two other pilot holes that are 1½-2" from the end of the outline. See figures 6-5 and 6-6 below.

Figure 6-5

TOP VIEW

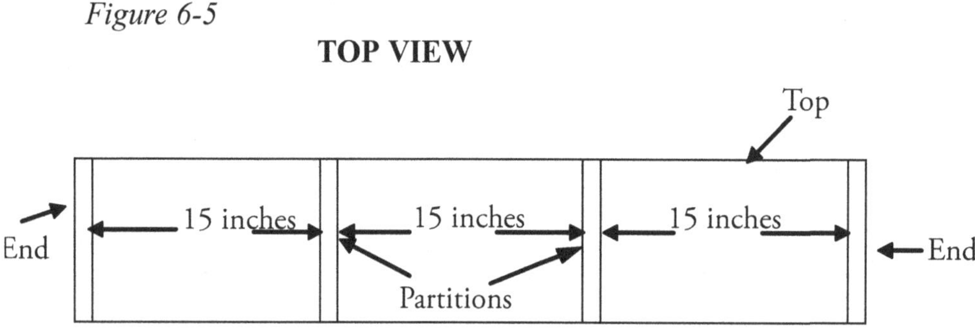

Figure 6-6

SIDE VIEW

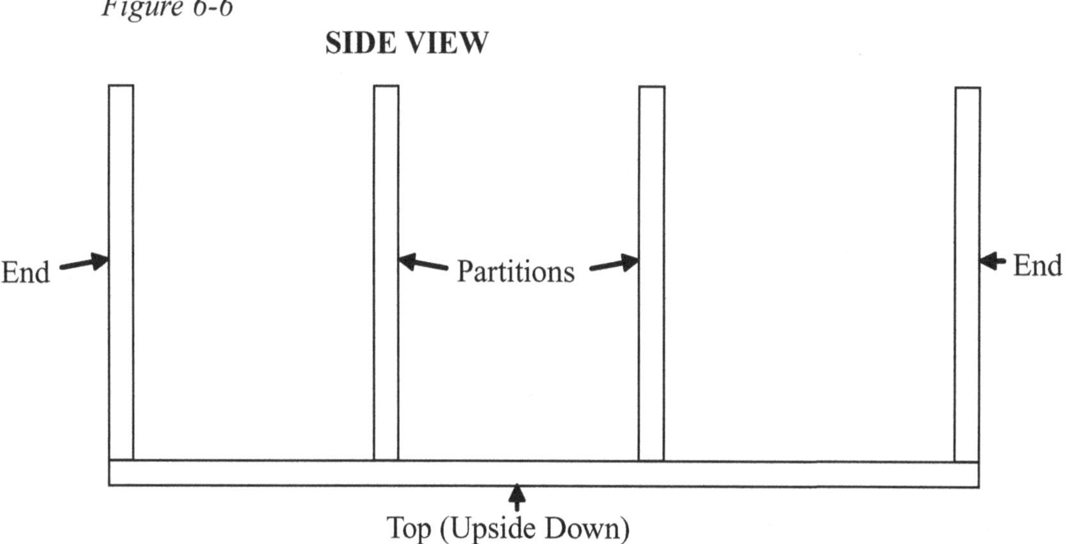

STEP 3. ASSEMBLY OF THE TOP, BOTTOM, ENDS, AND PARTITIONS

Assemble and fasten the *top*, 2 *ends*, and 2 *partitions* to the *bottom*. You may want to practice the assembly of the wood before fastening the pieces together. Make sure the pilot holes are lined up and that the *bottom*, 2 *ends*, 2 *partitions*, and *top* fit together the way you want them to. Remember that you want the mobile store to be square. Use a framing square or something that will help you make sure that the 2 *ends* and 2 *partitions* are square (form a 90 degree angle) to the *top* and *bottom*. Once you are satisfied with the pilot holes and where and how everything is going to fit together, you are ready to fasten the pieces together with glue and multipurpose screws. Assemble the six pieces like shown in the diagram below. Glue and screw all the places where 2 pieces of wood will be fastened together. Once you have glued and screwed the six pieces together, (*top*, *bottom*, 2 *ends*, 2 *partitions*) again, make sure they are square. Use a framing square or something equivalent. Wash off excess glue with a damp rag and allow glue to dry. See figure 6-7 below.

Figure 6-7

SIDE VIEW

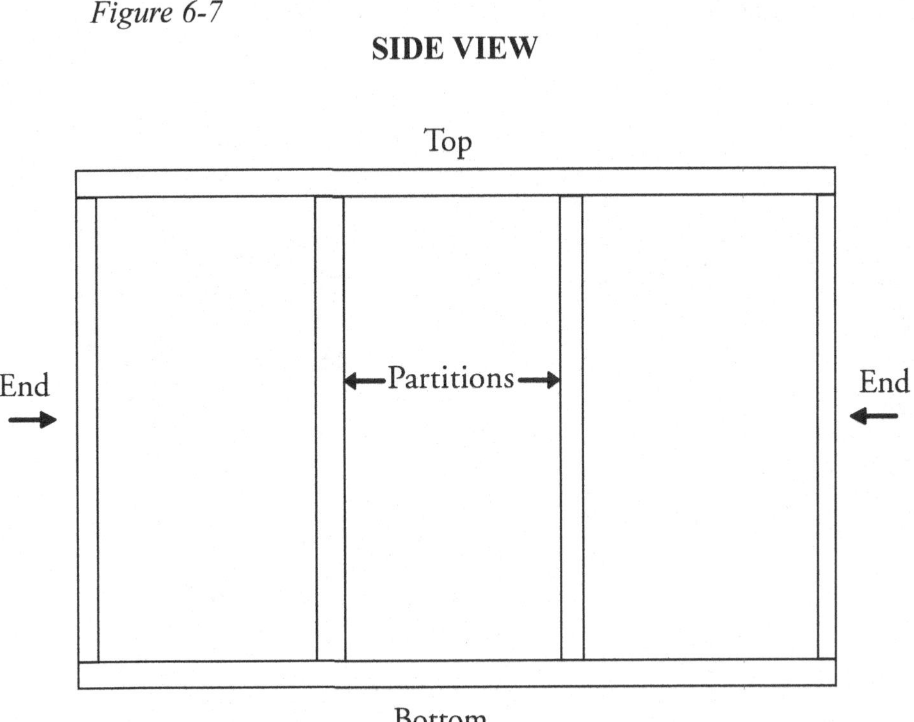

STEP 4. PAINT OR STAIN AND POLYURATHANE

Paint or stain and polyurethane the *top*, *bottom*, 2 *ends*, 2 *partitions, back 1,* and *back 2.* You may want to paint the store your school colors and/or add a logo or mascot. There are many possibilities. If you do not desire to paint or stain the school store, the natural wood looks great also.

STEP 5. FASTEN SHELF BRACKETS

Fasten the shelf brackets vertically to the 2 *ends* and 2 *partitions* with the nails that come in the bag of shelf clips. Each *end* and *partition* will have 2-36 inch shelf brackets vertically mounted on them on the inside of the store. The *ends* will have the shelf brackets on one side (the inside) and the *partitions* will have shelf brackets on both sides. The shelf brackets that are attached to the *ends* are fastened 2" from both edges of the *ends*. The shelf brackets fastened to the 2 *partitions* facing the 2 *ends* are also attached 2" from both edges of the *partitions*. The shelf brackets fastened to the *partitions* facing in toward each other are fastened 1 ½" from both edges. Figures 6-8 and 6-9 show examples of mounted shelf brackets.

Figure 6-8

Figure 6-9

STEP 6. CUTTING THE FRONT FROM THE ACRYLIC

Note: The pieces that are going to be cut and assembled are *italicized*. The piece for the *front* in figure 6-10 is not proportional to the whole sheet of Acrylic in the picture below. This was done to make the diagram easier to read.

When cutting the Acrylic, it is best to use a small-toothed saw blade. The Acrylic can be cut with a skill saw but a table saw will result in straighter cuts. Remember the saw blade is about 1/8-inch thick and has to be taken into consideration when cutting, so that the pieces don't end up too short, or not the correct size.

6a. Cut the Acrylic for the *front* of the store. You may want to re-measure to get the exact length and width for the *front* of the store before cutting. The dimensions below should be the correct size, depending on how precise you were in steps 1 through 3. It never hurts to double check the measurements. You could be off a sixteenth or eighth of an inch, which may or may not be a big deal. You can cut the acrylic to the exact dimensions desired so there is no overhang or undesired gaps. Figure 6-10 shows the length and width of the *front* of the store.

Figure 6-10

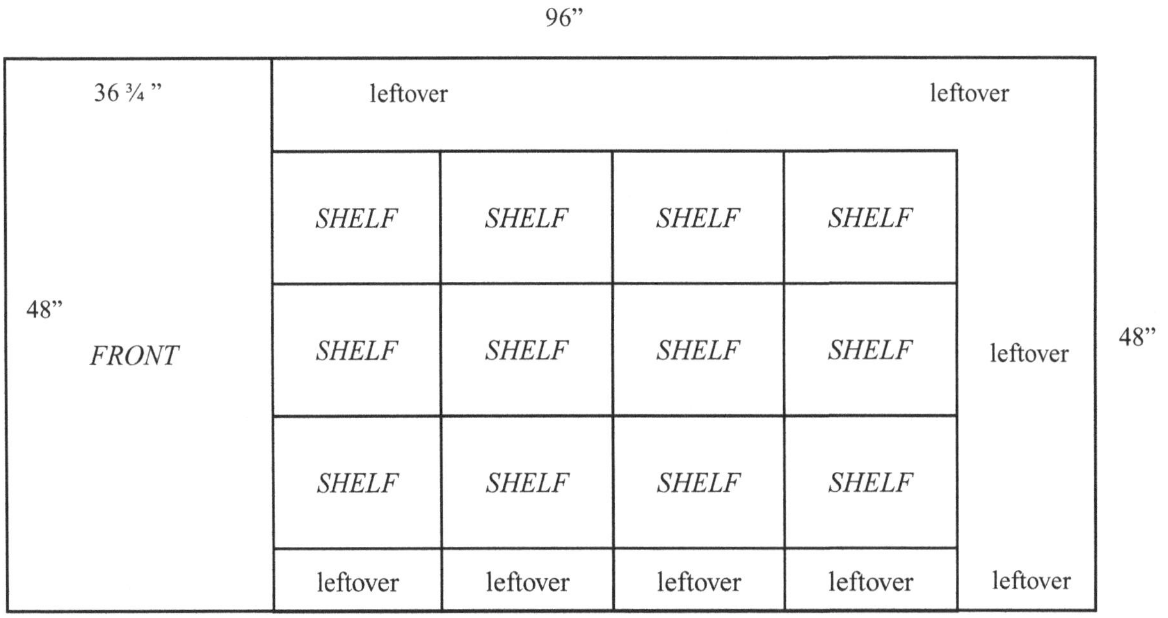

96"

36 ¾ "	leftover			leftover	
48" *FRONT*	*SHELF*	*SHELF*	*SHELF*	*SHELF*	
	SHELF	*SHELF*	*SHELF*	*SHELF*	leftover
	SHELF	*SHELF*	*SHELF*	*SHELF*	
	leftover	leftover	leftover	leftover	leftover

48"

STEP 7. PREPARATION AND FASTENING OF THE FRONT

Note: Acrylic can crack if not fastened properly. Therefore, pilot holes need to be drilled into the ¼" X 48" X 36 ¾" piece of Acrylic before it can be fastened to the *top*, 2 *ends*, and 2 *partitions*.

7a. To do this, set the piece of Acrylic that was just cut onto the front of the store where it is going to be fastened.

7b. Mark on the Acrylic, with a marking devise (magic marker), all the places where the *front* will be fastened to the *top*, 2 *ends*, and 2 *partitions*. It is recommended that you fasten about 24 pan-head screws, equally spacing them around the *top,* 2 *ends*, and 2 *partitions*. You may use more if desired.

7c. Once your fastening locations are marked remove the Acrylic from the front of the store and drill pilot holes through the Acrylic where your marks are. Keep the drill bit spinning fast and don't apply too much pressure at one time on the Acrylic when drilling pilot holes. The pilot holes need to be as big as the screw shaft, so that the screw shaft is free sliding through the Acrylic. After the pilot holes are drilled into the Acrylic, place the acrylic onto the front of the store. The Acrylic can be fastened with 1" to 1 ½" pan-head course thread wood screws, or whatever you feel is reasonable. You may also want to drill smaller pilot holes for the pan-head screws into the edges of the *top,* 2 *ends*, and 2 *partitions*.

7d. Fasten the *front* to the *top*, 2 *ends*, and 2 *partitions* of the school store. The Acrylic can be assembled like it is or it can be made more custom. If a more custom look is desired, take a drill bit bigger than the one you used to make pilot holes in the *front*. On each pilot hole, drill a small portion of the top of the hole with the larger drill bit. This will form a concave top in the holes and the screw will be able to be screwed in so that the top of the screw is flush with the face of the *front*. Or, the screws can stick out. Either looks fine.

When doing the final tightening of the screws you may want to use a screwdriver, so you don't over tighten and crack the *front* if you used a battery powered screw driver.

STEP 8. CUTTING THE SHELVES FROM THE ACRYLIC

When cutting the Acrylic, it is best to use a small-toothed saw blade. The Plexiglas/Acrylic can be cut with a skill saw but a table saw will result in straighter cuts. Remember the saw blade is about 1/8-inch thick and has to be taken into consideration when cutting, so that the pieces don't end up too short, or not the correct size.

8a. Now that your shelf brackets and the *front* are fastened, you can cut the *shelves* out of the remaining sheet of Acrylic. The size for the *shelves* depends on the shelf brackets and clips that you use. Each of the three columns may be slightly different depending on the assembly in steps 1 through 3, step 5, and the thickness of your shelf brackets and clips.

You know that the three columns that are going to have *shelves* should all be 12" deep (shelf length). You want a 1/16" space on the front and back of each *shelf* so that they aren't tight. 1/16 + 1/16 = 1/8. So, 12" - 1/8" = 11 7/8". Therefore, the length/depth of the *shelves* can be cut **11 7/8" deep.** However, remeasure and recheck with a tape measure to make sure you need exactly 11 7/8".

The width of the *shelves* has to be cut 1/8" (1/16 on each width side) less than the amount of space between the shelf brackets in that column, so that they aren't tight/pinched. For example, if the space between the shelf brackets in one of the columns is 14 ½", then the width of the *shelves* for that column is 14 ½" - 1/8" = **14 3/8" wide.**

Therefore, the *shelves* for that column would be **11 7/8" deep X 14 3/8" wide.** Figure 6-11 shows how the 12 *shelves* may be cut from the sheet of acrylic. **Remember to measure each column separately before you cut.**

Figure 6-11

36 ¾ "	leftover			leftover	
	SHELF	*SHELF*	*SHELF*	*SHELF*	
48" *FRONT*	*SHELF*	*SHELF*	*SHELF*	*SHELF*	leftover
	SHELF	*SHELF*	*SHELF*	*SHELF*	
	leftover	leftover	leftover	leftover	

STEP 9. ASSEMBLY OF THE CONTINUOUS HINGES TO BACK 1, BACK 2, AND THE TOP

9a. *Back 1* and *back 2* can be fastened together with one of the 48" continuous hinges. To do this, screw the hinge onto the edges of *back 1* and *back 2* with the hinge joint facing up. See figure 6-12 below.

Figure 6-12

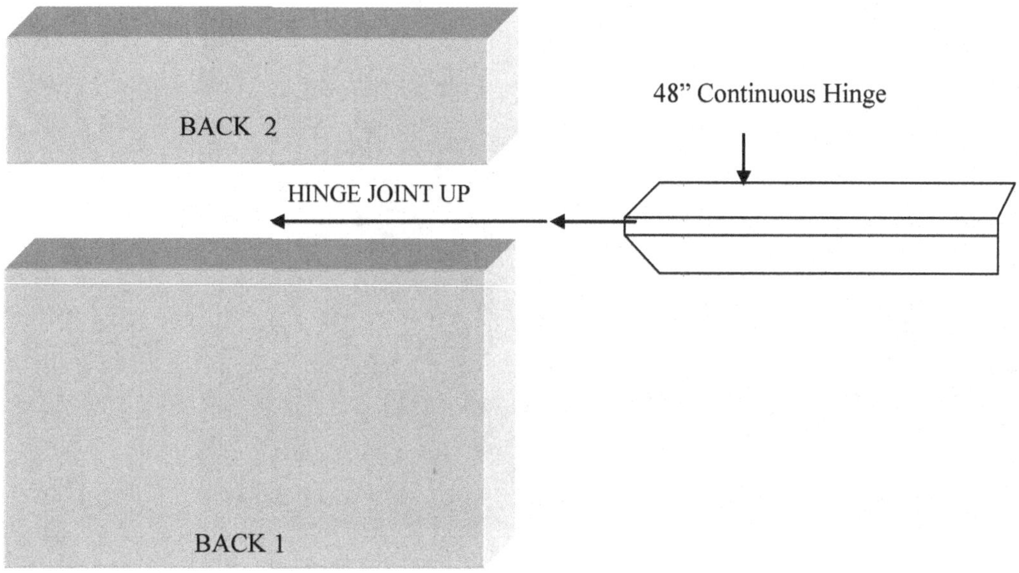

9b. After *back 1* and *back 2* are fastened together, fasten *back 2* to the edge of the *top* of the store with the second continuous hinge. Be sure the hinge joint faces down or in towards the body of the store. See figure 6-13 below.

Figure 6-13

After complete assembly and fastening of *back 1* and *back 2* to the edge of the *top* of the store, a side view will look like figure 6-13 and 6-14 when the store is closed.

Figure 6-14

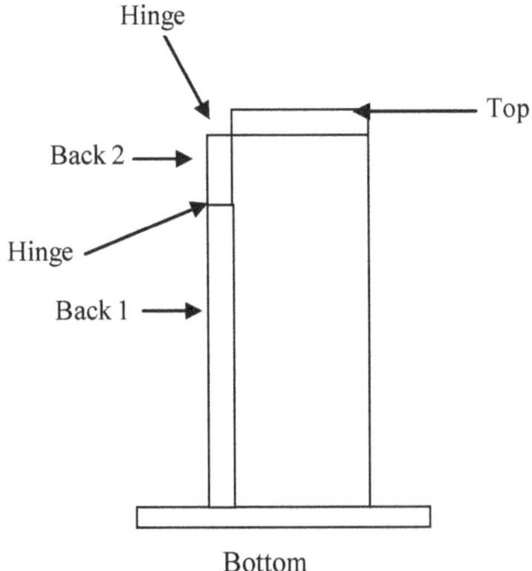

9c. After complete assembly and fastening of *back 1* and *back 2* to the edge of the *top* of the store, *back 1* flips up and rests on the *top* when the store is opening for business. See figures 6-15, 6-16, 6-17, 6-18, and 6-19.

Figure 6-15

Figure 6-16

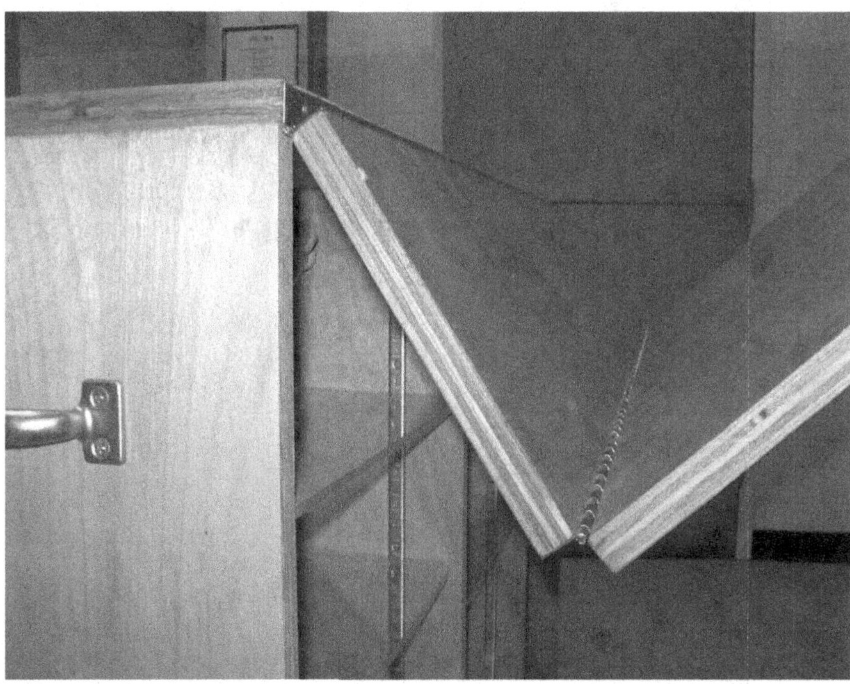

Figure 6-17

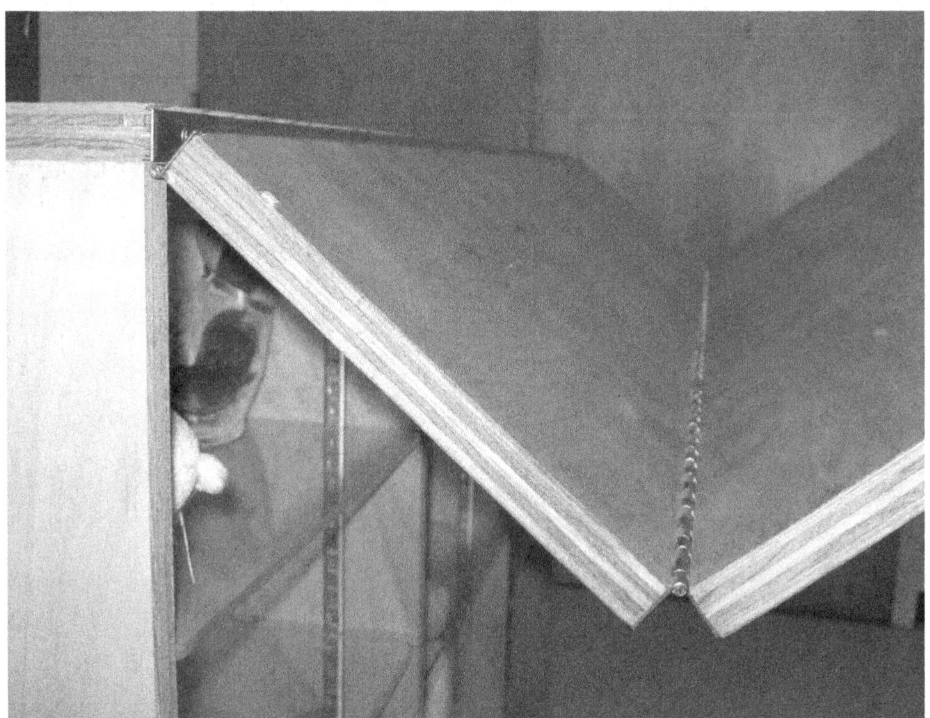

Figure 6-18

Figure 6-19

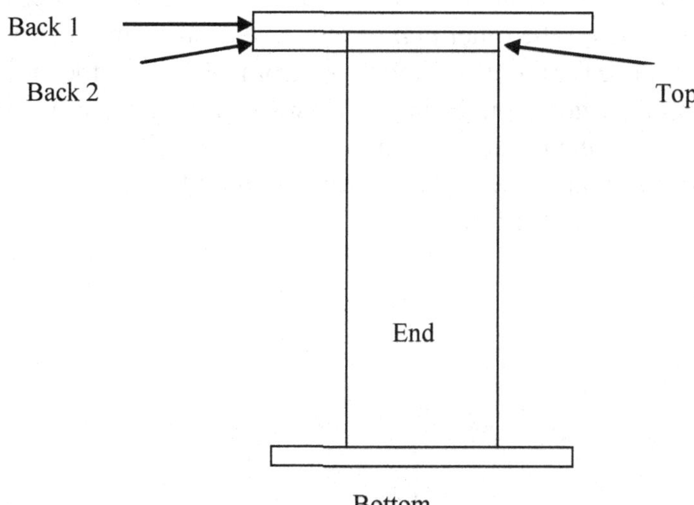

STEP 10. FASTEN HANDLES

Fasten handles with multipurpose screws to the outside *end* of the store where you feel is the best location. Fasten the second handle on the other *end* of the store in the same relative location. These handles will be used to move the mobile school store from location to location. Try not to have the screws to long so they go through the ¾" plywood and into the inside of the store. Students may get scratched when reaching for school supplies if the screws go through the ¾" plywood. The screws that come with the handle should be acceptable, however, double check for appropriate length. See figure 6-20.

Figure 6-20

STEP 11. FASTEN HASPS

Hasps have two parts. One piece is the hinge with the flap and the second piece is the loop bracket. When the flap is flipped onto the loop bracket, the hasp can secure something.

The hasps serve two purposes for the mobile store. The first purpose is to lock the school store when it is not in use. The second purpose is to secure *back 1* onto the *top* when *back 1* is flipped onto the *top* when you are open for business. Without securing the flap onto the loop bracket when the store is open, *back 1* may flip up if someone leans on the back of the *back 1* when they are selling items.

11a. Attach the hasps. To do this, flip *back 1* onto the *top* like in figures 6-21 and 6-22. Measure in about 9 inches from the front edge of *back 1* and fasten the hinge flap to *back 1* so that the hinge hangs down over the *end* of the store. Make sure the hinge joint is down or towards the body of the store. As the hinge flap hangs down onto the *end* of the store, note where the loop bracket should be placed so that the hinge flap goes over the loop bracket and secures *back 1* to the *top* of the store. The pictures and diagrams below show how *back 1* is secured to the *top* with a hasp. Do the same procedure on the other side of the store with another hinge flap and loop bracket.

Figure 6-21 (first side)

Figure 6-22(second side)

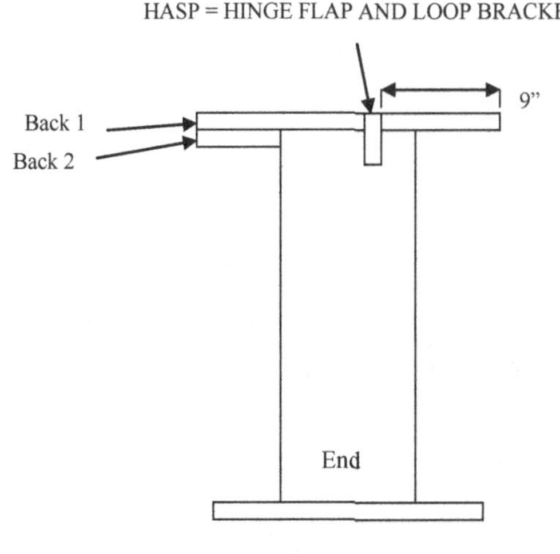

11b. Take the two other loop brackets out of their package and also fasten them to the end of the store. To do this, close *back 1* like you want to lock the store. Notice where the hinge flap lines up on the *end* so that the loop bracket can be fastened (about 9 inches from the bottom of the *end*). Do the same procedure to the other *end*. See figures 6-23 and 6-24. Figure 6-23 also includes a photo of a lock through the hasp assembly, locking and securing the mobile school store.

Figure 6-23

Figure 6-24

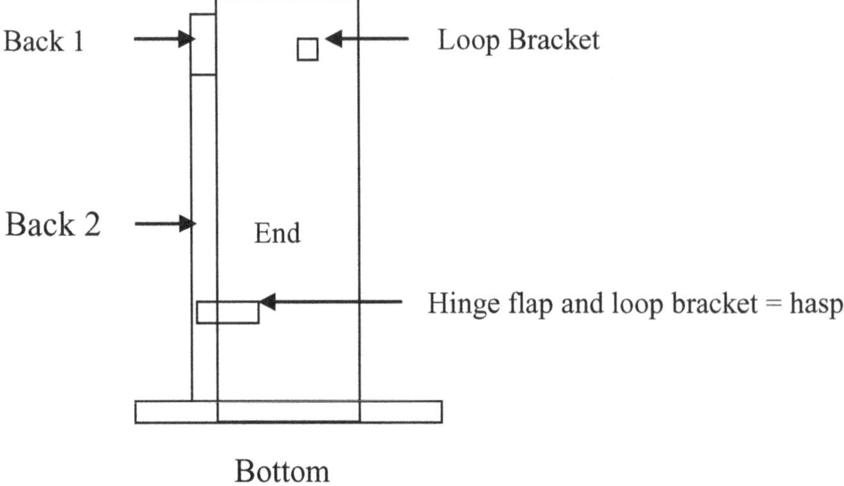

STEP 12. FASTEN CASTORS

12a. Holes need to be drilled into the *bottom* to fasten the castors. Therefore, after the hasps are secured, take out all the shelves and turn the store upside down and rest it on its *top*. Two fixed castors should be on one end of the *bottom* and the two swivel castors on the other end of the *bottom*. Line up the castors so that they are about an inch away from each of the edges and ends of the *bottom*. Make sure that wherever you line them up that the bolt being fastened won't be affecting the Acrylic or the *ends*. Next, mark where the holes should be drilled for the bolts to go through. After drilling holes, attach the castors to the *bottom* with bolts, lock washers and nuts. See figure 6-25 below.

Figure 6-25

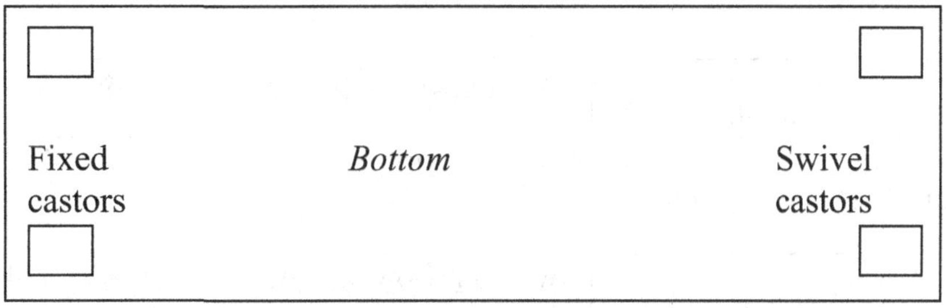

SECTION 7

ADDITIONAL RESOURCES

All resources listed were available when this book was written. Some of these resources may become expired in the future do to unforeseen reasons with the resource's website, e-mail, phone number, or company.

VENDORS WITH SUPPLIES

NAME / TYPE OF SUPPLY SITE	E-MAIL	PHONE
Student Supply / school supplies	www.studentsupply.com	1-800-426-6351
Didax Educational Resources/school supplies	www.didaxinc.com	1-800-458-0024
Max L. Cowen / school supplies	www.MaxCowen.com	1-800-874-4004
Staples	www.staples.com	1-800-STAPLES
School Specialty/school supplies	www.classroomdirect.com	1-800-248-9171
Oriental Trading Company Inc.	www.orientaltrading.com	1-800-228-2269
U.S. Toy Company	www.ustoy.com	1-800-832-0224
Miles Kimball	www.mileskimball.com	1-800-546-2255
The Learning Shop	www.learningshop.com	1-800-236-7467
Walmart	www.walmart.com	
Sam's Club	www.samsclub.com	

ENTREPRENEURSHIP ADDRESSES ON THE WEB (Websites for "E" Educators)

- http://www.aybc.org/
- www.sbaonline.sba.gov
- www.sba.gov/womeninbusiness/
- www.state.ne.us/
- www.census.gov
- www.ltbn.com
- www.entrepreneurmag.com
- www.fdncenter.org
- www.irs.ustreas.gov
- www.emkf.org

INTERNET MALLS

- www.21stcenturyplaza.com/ http://shopping.aol.com/coupons/

FOREIGN ENTREPRENEURSHIP PAGES

- www.cybf.ca/

MINORITY RESOURCES

- www.hispanstar.com/
- www.hispanstar.com/resrch/bizlinks.htm

OTHER RESOURCES

- www.sbaer.uca.edu/
- **The Institute for Entrepreneurship Phone: 773-794-2400**

RESOURSE SITES FOR TEACHERS

- http://www.ccsso.org
- http://www.kn.pacbell.com/wired/news/news.html
- http://www.edweek.org
- http://www.fastweb.com
- http://www.capecod.net/schrockguide/
- http://groups.google.com/groups?q=educational+resources&hl=en&lr=&ie=UTF-8&oe=UTF-8&selm=7gk36p%24spa%40spool.cs.wisc.edu&rnum=1
- http://groups.google.com/groups?q=educational+resources&hl=en&lr=&ie=UTF-8&oe=UTF-8&selm=65uhkq%2482r%40spool.cs.wisc.edu&rnum=2
- http://www.ecb.org/finance

LESSON PLAN SITES

- http://www.col-ed.org/cur/lang.html
- http://www.learner.org/exhibits/
- http://www.lessonplanspage.com/javaframe.htm
- www.TeachersNetwork.org
- www.google.com/apps/alloftheabove
- www.lessonopoly.org
- www.teachervision.fen.com/
- And many more. Just Google Teacher Lesson Plans

HOMEWORK ASSISTANCE WEBSITES

- http://www.geocities.com/ivonebl/
- http://www.bigchalk.com/cgi-bin/WebObjects/WOPortal.woa/db/Home.html

NOTES:

GLOSSARY

Academic Standards Standards that specify what students should know and be able to do (content), what they might be asked to do to give evidence of meeting standards (performance), and how well they must perform (proficiency).

Account Money deposited in a bank, savings account or checking account, which may be withdrawn by the depositor.

Asset Any item of value owned by a business (buildings, computers, inventory, and machinery are examples of assets).

Bank An institution which provides financial services including savings and checking accounts, loans and safety deposit boxes.

Bankrupt A term used to describe a business that is unable to pay it's bills and therefore unable to continue operating. A business declared legally bankrupt may have its assets or property confiscated by the court and divided among creditors.

Barter To trade a good or service with someone for a different good or service. No money is exchanged.

Budget A plan of how much money a person, business, government, or any organization has to spend and how it will spend it.

Business The buying and selling of goods and services in order to make a profit.

Check. A written order to a bank to pay a specific amount of money to a specific person or company. The money has been previously deposited in a checking account.

Checking Account. A bank account that may or may not earn interest, which the account holder can write checks from.

Competitive Advantage The features of a product or service that differentiate it from its competitors and make it better or more desirable.

Currency Any kind of money that is used to exchange goods for services.

Debt Money you owe when you purchase something on credit or borrow from someone else.

Default Not to pay back a loan.

Deposit To place money into a bank account.

Economy The way money flows into and out of a society.

Entrepreneur A person who organizes and manages a business, assuming the risk for the sake of the potential return.

Entrepreneurship Entrepreneurship is the process of planning and organizing a business or enterprise.

Equity Ownership in a company received in exchange for investment in the company. Equity is equal to assets minus liabilities.

Fee A fixed charge.

Finance To raise money for a business.

Fixed Costs Business expenses that must be paid whether or not any sales have occurred. Advertising, utilities, rent, insurance, and salaries are examples of fixed costs.

Free Enterprise System Economic system in which businesses are privately owned and operated relatively free of government control.

Goods Anything of some value, which may be traded for or purchased.

Gross. Total or entire amount before deductions.

Gross Profit The total sales revenue minus the cost of goods sold (sometimes expressed as margin or percent).

Gross Profit Per Unit The selling price minus the cost of goods sold of an item.

Imports. Goods brought into the country from abroad.

Incentive Something that motivates a person to take action. Financial rewards could be an incentive to work, start a business, or sell something. Buying something could be the incentive for filling a need.

Interest Payment for using someone else's money. Payment you receive for lending someone money.

Interest Rate A percentage per unit of time. Annual, monthly, compounded daily, etc.

Internal Revenue Service The federal government bureau in charge of taxation.

Installment Credit An arrangement between a store and a customer, which allows a purchase to be paid for in partial payments.

Installment Partial payment of a debt.

Loan Money borrowed for a certain amount of time, usually requiring the payment of interest to the lender by the borrower.

Management The art of planning, organizing, and running a business so it can meet its goals.

Manufacturing Making or producing a tangible product.

Market A group of people interested in buying a product or service. Situations where trade occurs.

Middlemen Word often used as substitute for "wholesaler." A trader who buys commodities from the producer or wholesaler and sells them to the retailer.

Money Anything a group of people accepts in exchange for goods or services.

Negotiation Discussing or bargaining in an effort to reach agreement between parties with differing goals.

Net Final. The profit or loss after all costs and taxes have been subtracted.

Operating Costs Each cost necessary to operate a business, not including cost of goods sold. Operating costs can almost always be divided into fixed and variable costs.

Overhead The continuing fixed costs of running a business. The costs a business has to pay in order to operate.

Partnership An association of two or more partners in a business enterprise.

Performance Standards Performance standards provide clear statements of the kinds of performances that constitute evidence that students had met the content standards. They answer the question, how well must a student perform.

Profit Money a business makes over the expenses of producing and selling its products.

Savings Money that is put somewhere safe so that it can be used later.

Service Any work that can be done for money or barter.

BIBLIOGRAPHY

Bilzing, D., & Colussy, C. (Winter, 1997-98). School to Work & Career Development. Wisconsin Department of Public Instruction.

International Consortium for Entrepreneurship Education. (Winter, 1994). EntrepreNews & Views: A New Venture in Vocational Education. (Vol 4, No. 1). Center on Education and Training for Employment The Ohio State University, Columbus, Ohio.

Jolin, J., & Randolph, R (1998). How to . . . Career Development Activities For Every Classroom (Grades K-3). University of Wisconsin-Madison. Center on Education and Work.

Jolin, J. & Randolph, R (1998). How to . . . Career Development Activities For Every Classroom (Grades 4-6). University of Wisconsin-Madison. Center on Education and Work.

Lindskog, M. (1997). Dollars and Sense. Grand Rapids, Michigan: Instructional Fair, TS Denison.

National Occupational Information Coordinating Committee. (1996). National Career Development Guidelines.
Center for Learning Connections. Highline Community College. Des Moines, WA.

Northern Lake Winnebago Private Industry Council. (1995). Youth Entrepreneur Program. State of Wisconsin
Division of Jobs, Employment, and Training Services.

Wisconsin Department of Public Instruction. (1987). A Guide to Curriculum Planning in Business Education. (Bulletin No. 7310). Milwaukee, WI. Publication Sales.

Wisconsin Department of Public Instruction. (1990). Education for Employment: A Resource and Planning Guide. (Bulletin No. 9160). Milwaukee, WI. Publication Sales.

Wisconsin Department of Public Instruction. (1999). Mentoring Youth for Success. (Bulletin No. 00054). Milwaukee, WI. Publication Sales

Wisconsin Department of Public Instruction. (1998). Wisconsin's Model Academic Standards for Business. (Bulletin No. 9004). Milwaukee, WI. Publication Sales.

Wisconsin Department of Public Instruction. (1998). Wisconsin's Model Academic Standards for English language arts. (Bulletin No. 8159). Milwaukee, WI Publication Sales.

Wisconsin Department of Public Instruction. (1997). Wisconsin's Model Academic Standards for Foreign Languages. (Bulletin No. 98032). Milwaukee, WI. Publication Sales.

Wisconsin Department of Public Instruction. (1998). Wisconsin's Model Academic Standards for Information & Technology Literacy. (Bulletin No. 9002). Milwaukee, WI. Publication Sales.

Wisconsin Department of Public Instruction. (1998). Wisconsin's Model Academic Standards for Marketing
Education. (Bulletin No. 9005). Milwaukee, WI. Publication Sales.

Wisconsin Department of Public Instruction. (1998). Wisconsin's Model Academic Standards for Mathematics. (Bulletin No. 8160). Milwaukee, WI. Publication Sales.

Wisconsin Department of Public Instruction. (1997). Wisconsin's Model Academic Standards for Music. (Bulletin No. 97309). Milwaukee, WI. Publication Sales.

Wisconsin Department of Public Instruction. (1997). Wisconsin's Model Academic Standards for Personal Financial Literacy. (Bulletin No. 98304). Milwaukee, WI. Publication Sales.

Wisconsin Department of Public Instruction. (1998). Wisconsin's Model Academic Standards for Science. (Bulletin No. 8161). Milwaukee, WI Publication Sales.

Wisconsin Department of Public Instruction. (1998). Wisconsin's Model Academic Standards for Social Studies. (Bulletin No. 8162). Milwaukee, WI. Publication Sales.

Wisconsin Department of Public Instruction. (1998). Wisconsin's Model Academic Standards for Technology Education. (Bulletin No. 9006). Milwaukee, WI. Publication Sales.

Wisconsin Department of Public Instruction. (1997). Wisconsin's Model Academic Standards for Theatre. (Bulletin No. 97308). Milwaukee, WI. Publication Sales.